Teaching
World
Understanding

Courtesy of *Farquhar Transparent Globes, Philadelphia,*
and The Philadelphia Inquirer

Teaching World Understanding

Edited by RALPH C. PRESTON

New York   PRENTICE-HALL, INC.   1955

PRENTICE-HALL EDUCATION SERIES

Editors

John S. Brubacher
Harold Spears

Contributors

ROBERT E. EATON
Teacher in Lower School, Germantown, Pennsylvania, Friends School

LUCINDA ILIFF
Teacher of history, Upper School, Germantown, Pennsylvania, Friends School

LEONARD S. KENWORTHY
Former teacher of social studies in Friends' schools; now Associate Professor of Education, Brooklyn College

MARY ESTHER McWHIRTER
Former Director of Children's Work, New York State Council of Churches, now Executive Secretary, Committee on Educational Materials for Children, American Friends Service Committee

RALPH C. PRESTON
Professor of Education, University of Pennsylvania

DAVID S. RICHIE
Former teacher of social studies, Moorestown, New Jersey, Friends School; now Executive Secretary, Social Order Committee, Philadelphia Yearly Meetings of the Religious Society of Friends, and director of various work camp programs, Philadelphia and abroad

ERNEST F. SEEGERS
Chairman, History Department, George School

GEORGE A. WALTON
Principal Emeritus, George School; former Co-Director, School Affiliation Service, American Friends Service Committee; now Chairman, Friends General Conference

Preface

This book describes tested procedures for developing understanding of the peoples of the world among young Americans. All the authors are or have been affiliated with Quaker schools and other Quaker educational agencies and have drawn freely upon these experiences in preparing their respective chapters. Quakers, of course, have no monopoly of knowledge or skill in the area of educating for world understanding, and, as indicated in the text, some of the ideas, procedures, and illustrations of practices described are of non-Quaker origin. Yet *Teaching World Understanding* could hardly have been written without the long experimentation in educating for world understanding that Quaker education has always encouraged.

Proceeding from the basic Quaker tenet that at heart there is something of God in every man, Quaker educational agencies have as a major objective the development of a deep respect for human personality wherever and however it may be found. This, they believe, is the basis of world citizenship. "The inhabitants of the earth," wrote John Woolman, prominent eighteenth century American Quaker, "have often appeared to me as one great family. . . . To consider mankind otherwise than brethren . . . plainly supposes a darkness of understanding." Throughout the 300 years of their existence,

Quakers have sought to impart this concept to children and youth.

This book was planned by the Friends Peace Committee of the Philadelphia Yearly Meetings of the Religious Society of Friends. A subcommittee, consisting of Frances Richardson, Stanley R. Yarnall, and Ralph C. Preston, chairman, was appointed to "study what is being done through Quaker education..." The idea of the book grew from their study. The subcommittee was later enlarged by the addition of Frances Haviland and F. Palin Spruance, Jr. The subcommittee engaged Eleanor Spruance to collect information about practices relating to education for world understanding by visiting the Quaker schools in the Philadelphia region. The authors of the various chapters have had access to this survey material and have also drawn upon their own experiences as participants in Quaker and other educational enterprises. The authors have also utilized their familiarity with practices in public and non-Quaker private schools in the United States and Europe.

The aim of those engaged in this enterprise has been to construct a volume offering description, encouragement, and practical suggestions to the increasing number of teachers who are seeking to develop in children and youth an understanding of world cultures which will help prepare them to work effectively as adults toward a warless world.

The subcommittee is indebted to the former and the present executive secretaries of the Friends Peace Committee, Richard R. Wood and George C. Hardin, for their constant help, and the editor is indebted to his wife, Madeline P. Preston, for invaluable editorial assistance.

RALPH C. PRESTON
University of Pennsylvania

Contents

ix

Contents

Teaching World Understanding

1

Issues in Teaching World Understanding

RALPH C. PRESTON

Thoughtful educators are conscious of a heavy task
which the times have imposed upon them. That task is
to see that the young people of this generation acquire
world understanding—that is, a sympathetic acquaintance and
a feeling of kinship with the peoples of other lands.

Educators in increasing numbers are looking for ways to
accomplish this end. Yet some teachers are beset by doubts
which thwart their efforts. "Are we fooling ourselves," they
ask, "when we think our efforts at enlightenment really overcome prejudice? And when we do go to work on attitudes, are
we not stepping down as educators and assuming the role of
propagandists?" The present chapter considers these and other
doubts and suggests their resolution. Later chapters give some
workable answers to these doubts.

This chapter is written in the belief that a teacher, before
being able to help create in his pupils world understanding
based on integrity and a feeling of security, will need to face

I

Figure 1. Visitor from Indonesia reads to some five-year-olds. Courtesy of Oak Lane Country Day School, Philadelphia.

the issues raised by his doubts and know where he stands on each of them.

TO WHAT EXTENT CAN ATTITUDES BE CHANGED?

"It is hopeless to try to buck the prejudice of the home," is a common complaint of teachers. This, indeed, seems true when one's pupils have firmly opinionated parents who believe that foreigners are inferior and who maintain strong bonds of authority in the home. Every experienced teacher has tasted defeat in his effort to broaden the understanding and sympathies of certain children. Research has shown that the biased individual who identifies himself with some cause, or who exhibits hostility toward authority, is especially resistant to change. Such bias frequently relates to personal conflict and insecurity, and may have been adopted in response to an inner emotional need. In such cases, prejudice is well-rooted.

On the other hand, children are not born with prejudices; they acquire them. Furthermore, research has shown that we can inculcate desirable attitudes. Arnold M. Rose, in a review of nine studies designed to change attitudes toward minorities, finds seven of the studies succeeded in doing so; of eleven studies of classroom programs more educational and less propagandistic than the foregoing, he cites six which were successful. (*Studies in Reduction of Prejudice*, 1948.) We may conclude that education sometimes misses fire, but that attitudes *can* be altered. This is not news for teachers who have discovered that presentation of information in a classroom atmosphere of enthusiasm, inquiry, and mutual respect may be highly effective. Such an atmosphere is all-important. It must be one which engenders a spirit of open-minded inquiry in *all* matters—not only those pertaining to other cultures. It must be an atmosphere that encourages young people to discover facts for themselves. It must be penetrated by mutual regard and fair play. In a word, "good attitudes are promoted by everything that enables the child to make good emotional adjustments." (Arthur T. Jersild, *Child Development and the Curriculum*, 1946, p. 119. For other data on conditions favorable to attitude

3

change, see Carl I. Hovland *et al.*, *Communication and Persuasion: Psychological Studies of Opinion Change*, 1953.)

Such a classroom atmosphere breeds maturity. Maturity, in turn, breeds world understanding. Conversely, narrow, twisted attitudes toward other peoples are symptoms of immaturity. The teacher's fundamental task in broadening attitudes, therefore, is to make it easy for his pupils to grow up. As H. A. Overstreet points out, the teacher's own behavior is crucial: he must prize the give-and-take of teacher-pupil conversation and encourage pupil participation in school decisions. "Adults who speak only to deliver the final word of truth and authority are no fit companions for children." (*The Mature Mind*, 1949, p. 241.)

Almost every experienced teacher has had the keen satisfaction of seeing the narrow outlooks of certain pupils expand and their intolerance soften. But, unfortunately, teachers suffer from a kind of occupational disease which might be called magnification of failure. Too many of them are perfectionists, hoping, unrealistically, to influence in marked fashion every pupil in every class. These teachers are not quite sure of themselves. The mature teacher is confident of his general success because of his skill and the large number of pupils he serves. But he does not expect to influence all with equal results. He knows that some pupils are not ready to modify their prejudice, and he knows that some of the seeds he sows which do not sprout at once, may do so later on. Knowledge of these facts, as possessed by the mature teacher, does not make him diminish his effort with each pupil, but does give him perspective. Free from the fear of failure, he becomes more alert to signs of the first stirrings of a new outlook in his charges. He conserves his energies and emotions through being spared insecurity and disillusion.

IS TEACHING WORLD UNDERSTANDING
A FORM OF PROPAGANDA?

Many teachers shy away from teaching programs that have a tang of preaching about them, even for so worthy a cause as a warless world. Their point of view is that a teacher's function is to organize and present data, not to shape attitudes. Such teachers are to be commended for their integrity and their scrupulous avoidance of the spirit of propaganda in their teaching. If teaching world understanding involved the manipulation of the minds of children, and if it involved suppressing some of the facts and presenting only those favorable to the goal, then such teaching would, of course, be undesirable. It would express contempt for true education.

Yet true education is not always neutral. The social sciences are studded with value elements, including the basic assumption that personality is sacred and entitled to protection and respect. Without such value assumptions, any teaching of history, geography, or civics becomes sterile. For we are not simply concerned with discovering the facts; we are also wondering how they could be utilized to improve world conditions. It is here that cold, objective thinking leaves us in the lurch and value criteria come to the rescue.

In searching for a value criterion, how should the teacher proceed? Today, many a teacher is thinking about how we can improve international relations. No responsible teacher should evade such consideration, but neither should he seize upon some capricious or glittering panacea. He will search for a promising concept which has strong roots and has been

5

examined seriously and approved by thoughtful and wise men through the ages, and which rings true to his own best self. For instance, many who have thus searched have discovered impressive validity in the concept of the universal community, with its beginnings in the great religious teachers and embodied in organized plans. Formulators of such plans include Grotius, Penn, von Suttner, Wilson, and the architects of today's United Nations.

If a teacher espouses world understanding, he will be called by some people a propagandist. It is true he seeks to communicate a vision to his pupils. But there need not be, in the process, exploitation of the child, or distortion, suppression, or biased selection of facts. To the contrary, the teacher should set aside his own prejudices, dig out all available and relevant facts, and help his pupils explore them. The spirit, methods, and integrity of the teacher determine whether he is propagandist or educator.

DOES WORLD UNDERSTANDING CONFLICT WITH PATRIOTISM?

"The world is my country, all mankind are my brethren," wrote the eloquent American patriot, Thomas Paine. And countless loyal Americans since his time also have been swept by feelings of world citizenship. Yet teachers who emphasize the world view are sometimes accused of damaging their pupils' patriotism. The antagonism and suspicion of groups and individuals in this country who criticize the teaching of world understanding are probably often an emotional reaction to the poisoning and exploiting of a number of international movements by the Soviet Union to further its doctrinaire and nationalistic aims.

To be sure, it would be futile to try to create love of the entire world if love of one's own country were not well-rooted first. Dorothy Thompson has pointed out that patriotism is actually the basis of internationalism. Patriotism "is a feeling that binds mankind," she writes. "Precisely *because* I love my country I appreciate the love of others for *their* countries . . . I do not have to share their love for and allegiance to their particular object. But I am compelled to respect it . . ." Miss Thompson reminds us that those who have achieved world-wide acclaim—such as Shakespeare, Dante, Goethe, Dostoevsky, Mark Twain—"are precisely those who are most deeply rooted and immersed in their *own* culture." (*Ladies' Home Journal*, June, 1951, p. 14. Copyright 1951, The Curtis Publishing Company.)

The issue is not one of patriotism versus world citizenship. The question is, *how* can we teach patriotism and, at the same time, develop responsible attitudes toward foreign peoples? The first part of our job is to inculcate knowledge of our country, pride in it, and respect for the best in our national environment, aspirations, and traditions, and a wish to improve our country. The remaining portion of our job is to build a feeling of concern for the welfare of those in other nations. Such concern must underlie any kind of effective international organization. We should point the way to a world in which, to quote Arnold J. Toynbee, there is "a free consent of free peoples to dwell together in unity, and to make, uncoerced, the far-reaching adjustments and concessions without which this ideal cannot be realized in practice." (*A Study of History*, abridged edition, 1947, p. 552.)

Toynbee makes a strong case for the elimination of what he calls the "pagan worship" of national sovereignty in order to permit the development of international cooperation on a vast scale and to spare our civilization "annihilation by a knock-out blow." (Chapter 4.)

The present period is not the first one in history in which circumstances have prodded men to broaden their loyalties. In 1776, for example, our forefathers found it necessary to extend their loyalty from Colony to Confederation. Yet it is clear this enlargement of loyalty did not impair their pride in, or love for, their own respective Colonies. They simply recognized, with Benjamin Franklin, that "We must all hang together, or assuredly we shall all hang separately."

This is a blunt fact which, we are gradually learning, faces us again today in a new guise. The values of patriotism remain as vital as ever, and it is for the very purpose of protecting them that teachers should actively search out paths which lead to increased world understanding.

DOES EMPHASIS UPON WORLD UNDER-STANDING PROVIDE A MEANS FOR EVADING PERSONAL PROBLEMS?

Some teachers are sobered to such an extent by the present world crisis and the implications of the atom and hydrogen bombs that they become reformers, impatient with both the gradualness of a young person's growth and the gradualness of human progress. Thus, they cease to be real teachers. They try, unwisely, to superimpose the one-world concept on children and youth who have not yet achieved successful social relations in their own small spheres. World citizenship, love of humanity, and similar abstractions may become forms of escape for maladjusted pupils. Instances of such maladjustment have been noted in pacifist groups, for instance—indi-

8

viduals who love "humanity" but are at constant odds with their neighbors.

Sensitive teachers have seen this happen and have become worried. They fear, and rightly, that boys and girls who are not learning to conquer conflicts within themselves and with their associates are scarcely growing into adults who will contribute to either national or international harmony. Nor, they realize, are these children in a favorable psychological condition for the development of the "we" spirit and qualities such as openmindedness and integrity—the building blocks for any kind of international cooperation. Arthur E. Morgan has pointed out: "Personal character is the first essential for social usefulness . . . Crisis is always with us, and always is an excuse for evading the basic process of civilization: the refining, mastering, and developing of our own lives and intimate social relationships." (*Antioch Notes,* March 15, 1948, pp. 1 and 3.)

However, a teacher does not have to choose between building social vision on one hand and building mature personal character on the other. He can do both. By acquainting children and youth with the cultures of other countries and showing how interesting and stimulating it is that people's ways are not the same the world over, and how dull it would be if they were, he can help to broaden their outlook and increase their knowledge.

Children and youth may gain enrichment from national and cultural diversity. They may gain a measure of understanding of foreign peoples from the similarity of all peoples in their basic needs and reactions. Teaching should proceed with these aims in mind. Such teaching should also embody attention to the development of integrity in reporting facts, respect for the views of others, a habit of postponing judgment until sufficient

9

facts are at hand, and sheer ability to get along well with others.

CAN CONFIDENCE AND OPTIMISM BE BUILT IN A WAR-THREATENED WORLD?

A newspaper carries the headline: UNITED NATIONS MARKS BIRTHDAY BUT HAS NO CAUSE FOR CELEBRATION. It sometimes seems as though pessimism dominates our times, filling the very air. It is easily understood, therefore, why teachers often despair of building confident, optimistic attitudes in the learner regarding the future. Adolescents particularly have spells of pessimism. "Tomorrow who knows, today who cares" they ask with a shrug. "Peace is a lost cause," says one. "War is a law of nature," comments another. The teacher who wishes to build a vision of a warless world and the understanding needed to help bring it about often feels that he faces a mountain of hopelessness, helplessness, and cynicism.

Preaching sweetness and light is of no value—in fact, preaching of any kind is not the answer. Perhaps the best approach is patient, gentle, yet persistent and unremitting reference to certain important established facts. Four of these facts are:

1. *Progress toward world order has taken place.* The beginnings of world order can be traced as far back as Hugo Grotius, the Dutch jurist of the seventeenth century, who made the first formulation of international law, and the step-by-step progress since then of the united-world concept can be cited right down to the present in the functioning of the United Nations. The shortcomings of this body should not blind us to its tremendous significance. The magnitude of

creative thinking within the past 15 years about practical measures to bring about world order is in itself a substantial milestone of progress. Not the least encouraging aspect is that much of this creative thinking has come from concerned lay citizens. Some of these thoughtful, internationally-minded people are Bernard Baruch, Grenville Clark, Ely Culbertson, Clarence Streit, and Wendell Willkie.

2. *Pessimism is often caused by nearsightedness and poor perspective.* Quotations can be extracted from almost any period to verify this statement. Thus, Pitt said at the close of the eighteenth century: "There is scarcely anything around us but ruin and despair." And Wilberforce stated at the beginning of the nineteenth century: "I dare not marry, the future is so dark and unsettled." Pessimists point to the fact that today most of our energy and resources are going to the making and maintaining of armaments. We should know that fact and be dismayed by it, yet not overlook the growth of constructive values and the promise for a better life contained in contemporary developments. Encouraging discoveries and inventions for the betterment of society are well known, but need greater emphasis. For example, "incurable" mental disorders can now be successfully treated, the polio virus has been isolated, the smoke nuisance of manufacturing cities can now be reduced, disappearing wild life can be preserved, the productivity of an acre of soil has been increased, and techniques for mass production have increased the leisure of millions.

An increasing interest in the arts is a hopeful sign. In the field of music, the large outlay for classical records is worth noting, plus the tremendous number of symphony orchestras springing up in the United States in the past ten or fifteen years. The upsurge of interest in visual art is seen by the large attendance at exhibits and art museums, the number of exhibits shown, and the number of prints of famous paintings sold in stores and museums.

Publishers' statistics are often arresting and suggestive. For example, more Bibles were purchased in the past 15 years than in the past half century. Books on religion have been on best-selling lists in recent years. Constructive books like *Peace of Mind* and *The Mature Mind* have been best-sellers, showing public interest in improvement of individual personality and in group relationships. Slowly but surely people seem to be improving their attitudes toward their brothers. Examples of this trend are improved labor-management relations and reduction of racial and other intergroup tensions in this country.

International politics are showing improvement in some directions under the aegis of the United Nations. Ralph J. Bunche, who knows at first hand the frustrations and disappointments of the United Nations in its difficult tasks, can still affirm that, had there been no United Nations, "we almost certainly would have been in atomic World War III long ago . . . It has done few things perfectly, but in intervening in every threatening dispute it has put the brakes on and has tended to divert the use of force." (Quoted in *The New York Times*, September 13, 1953.)

Teachers should regularly collect and systematically file all such data for use in documenting for their pupils the thesis that there are, after all, grounds for optimism.

3. *Cooperation is a law of nature.* Theories about man's "innate fighting instinct," and the cliché that war is nature's law have gained wide and uncritical acceptance. What is needed in our schools is a vigorous presentation of the scientific evidence concerning human nature and what Clyde

12

Kluckhohn, the anthropologist, calls the "boundless plasticity" of human nature.

What have scientific investigators concluded? After reviewing the research on children's cooperative and aggressive behavior, Arthur T. Jersild points out that the findings "suggest that the potentialities for friendly, cooperative behavior are as strong as, or perhaps stronger, than the potentialities for behavior that involves self-assertion at the expense of or in opposition to others." (*Child Psychology*, 1954, p. 231.) A standard sociology textbook states: "Original nature does not dictate any single type of fighting nor does it determine that fighting shall occur with any definite frequency, or indeed that it shall occur at all." (William F. Ogburn and Meyer F. Nimkoff, *Sociology*, 1946, p. 53.) A group of thirteen distinguished psychologists maintain: "*War can be avoided: war is not born in men; it is built into men.* No race, nation or social group is inevitably warlike. The frustrations and conflicting interests which lie at the root of aggressiveness can be reduced and redirected by social engineering. Men can realize their ambitions within the framework of human cooperation and can direct their aggressiveness against those natural obstacles that thwart them in the attainment of their goals." (Gardner Murphy, editor, *Human Nature and Enduring Peace*, 1945, p. 455.)

Scientists have also addressed themselves to the popular belief that man has always waged war and hence war is inevitable. Clyde Kluckhohn, while warning that authorities are not fully agreed, observes: "It is not certain that warfare existed during the Old Stone Age. The indications are that it was unknown during the earlier part of the New Stone Age in Europe and the Orient . . . Organized, offensive warfare was unknown in Aboriginal Australia. Certain areas of the New World seem to have been completely free from war in the pre-European period." (*Mirror for Man: The Relation of Anthropology to Life*, 1949, p. 55. Copyright 1949 by McGraw-Hill Book Company, Inc.) Another prominent anthropologist, the late Bronislaw Malinowski, writes that "war can only be defined as the use of organized force between two politically independent units, in pursuit of tribal policy. War in this sense enters fairly late into the development of human societies." ("Culture as a Determinant of Behavior," Harvard Tercentenary Conference, *Factors Determining Human Behavior*, 1937, p. 141.)

Aside from familiarizing children and youth with such findings, teachers need also to call attention to what man has accomplished through voluntary cooperative endeavor—in harvesting crops, in building industry, in forming cooperatives and labor unions, in worshiping, in carrying out research, in exploring, and in countless other enterprises which have moved mankind forward. To be sure, most children know something about these activities at an early age, but they are inclined to take them for granted and the facts remain as random fragments of knowledge. It is the task for teachers to examine with their pupils these samples of man's cooperative drives in relation to the dangerous myth that man is equipped and doomed by nature for war.

4. *Each person's influence is important.* In answer to a high-school student's inquiry about the most important contribution students can make toward world peace, Bernard Baruch replied: "Do not think you're a zero, that you don't count. That's defeatism . . . No matter where you are, no matter what your position is, no matter how small you may think it is,

use your influence not alone to learn the truth but to teach it to others." (*Look*, July 31, 1951, p. ii.) Individuals who have had tremendous influence on their country and the world have not been so rare but that every teacher could name a dozen and could easily locate the biographies of a dozen others in any library. These histories of influential lives may be used to help young people learn that even they, small though they may feel in relation to the world they live in, can influence others. By such activities as talking, writing, contributing to causes, and associating with organized groups an individual can help to convince others of the validity of his ideas.

CONCLUSION

The issues discussed in this chapter are easier of resolution on paper than in practice. It is encouraging to note, however, that despite obstacles and doubts many teachers are meeting the great demand of our times to bring the peoples of the world closer in understanding. They know that without this greater understanding it is unlikely that the step from world anarchy to world order, and from there to world peace, can be accomplished. Teachers recognize, moreover, that the problem is as much educational in nature as political, and that they have it within their power as teachers to make a major contribution to the building of a safer, saner, kindlier world.

SUGGESTED READING

Anderson, Howard R., editor. *Approaches to an Understanding of World Affairs*. Twenty-fifth Yearbook of the National Council for the Social Studies. Washington, D. C.: National Council for the Social Studies, 1954.

Bryson, Lyman *et al.*, editors. *Approaches to World Peace: A Symposium.* New York: Conference on Science, Philosophy and Religion, 1944.

Klineberg, Otto. *Tensions Affecting International Understanding: A Survey of Research.* New York: Social Science Research Council, 1950.

Kluckhohn, Clyde. *Mirror for Man: The Relation of Anthropology to Life.* New York: Whittlesey House, 1949.

Meiklejohn, Alexander. *Education Between Two Worlds.* New York: Harper, 1942.

Murphy, Gardner, editor. *Human Nature and Enduring Peace.* Third Yearbook of the Society for the Psychological Study of Social Issues. Boston: Houghton Mifflin, 1945.

Rose, Arnold M. *Studies in Reduction of Prejudice.* Chicago: American Council on Race Relations, 1948.

Washburne, Carleton. *The World's Good: Education for World-Mindedness.* New York: John Day, 1954.

2

Studying Other Countries and Peoples in the Elementary School

LEONARD S. KENWORTHY

*P*arents and teachers know how difficult it is to help
boys and girls to learn to live with the children and
adults in their immediate environment, adjusting to the
slight degrees of differences which exist between persons in
the same society. They can therefore appreciate the much
more difficult task of helping boys and girls to understand and
appreciate the children and adults of other countries, who
have much more marked differences from themselves.

Yet a beginning at least must be made in the elementary
school before attitudes are formed which tend to be held for
life, before misinformation is accepted which will be difficult
to replace, and before habits are developed which it will be
almost impossible to unlearn. As the Educational Policies Commission has pointed out, "The elementary schools that will
make the greatest contribution to life in the next generation

Figure 2. A fifth grade studies Africa.

will be those schools that are related to the world community, yet are anchored firmly in their home community." (*Education for All American Children*, 1948, p. 279.)

THE WORLD COMMUNITY IN WHICH WE LIVE

A six-course dinner was recently given at the Commercial Club in San Francisco with the food for each course flown in that day by airlines from six different parts of the world. This was a dramatic way of demonstrating the kind of world in which we teachers and our pupils live today.

A turn of the knob on the radio or television, a glance at the date lines on the front page of any reputable newspaper, or a view of the newsreel in any theater will illustrate quickly the fact that we live in an air age, an atomic age, a troublous, changing, global world.

Our neighbors are no longer just the people who live next door or down the street. They are the people who live in China, India, and Korea; in Argentina, Mexico, and Uruguay; in England, Germany, and the U.S.S.R.; in Egypt, Israel, and Iran; in Australia, New Zealand, and the United States of Indonesia. Our community today is the world; our neighbors the two and a half billion persons on this planet.

Such an extension of our concept of community demands changes in the elementary-school curriculum. Pupils must still be taught how to live with their families, with their school-mates, with people in the local community and in the United States. They must also be taught how to live with their new neighbors in the world community.

And what a complex community it is, with its peoples of many nationalities, many religions, many colors, many stages of industrialization, many value systems, many political and economic orientations, and many ways of living!

POINTS OF EMPHASIS IN STUDYING OTHER COUNTRIES AND PEOPLES

The geographer, J. Russell Smith, once reminded teachers that "There are two enduring things that you may hope to plant in the minds or spirits of children. The most important of these that endure is attitude. Attitudes help to decide how we interpret the facts of life. Attitudes are perhaps the most important residue (after thirty years). The second important residue ... may be a few big ideas about countries, peoples, and places." (*Journal of Geography*, March, 1947, p. 101.)

What, then, are some of the attitudes and big ideas about other countries and peoples which elementary-school teachers should strive to develop?

First of all, children should learn that they live in a world of different kinds of people. This is an extension on the world scale of a concept which children can learn in their community. They need to realize that people are fundamentally the same the world over and that there are few basic, biological differences. At the same time they should begin to understand that differences do exist in the way people look, live, and think, and that such differences are often valuable, bringing enrichment to the world, just as differences between children in a classroom can make it a more interesting place.

Second, children should learn that people are affected by their environment and by the ways of living and thinking of their parents and other adults. It can be an exciting and important experience for children to see a movie like *Nomads of the Jungle* (United World Film, 1948) and discover how cleverly the children of the Malayan Peninsula have learned to adjust to their environment; or for boys and girls to try to figure out what they would do if they lived in a rocky, mountainous country like Norway. This is a part of the process of learning how people are affected by their environment and how they in turn alter the environment.

Likewise, children can begin to understand how boys and girls in every country learn from their parents and other adults how to act. The American boy may think the French boy who wears gloves on Sunday a "sissy," but he can learn that all French boys do this when paying a formal visit, and that *all* gentlemen do this in France, whether they are prize fighters or diplomats. This is a simple illustration of the begin-

20

ning of understanding how people acquire manners and customs, whether in Philadelphia, Paris, or Persepolis.

Third, children should learn that countries are very much like people and are affected by their size, location, history, and beliefs. Although there are dangers in such an analogy, it is probably one of the easiest ways of helping children to understand the different nations of the world and how they act. Children can think of small countries and large countries, old countries and young countries, and even relatively happy countries and relatively unhappy countries. They can begin to understand why a nation with centuries of history like China often acts differently from a young country like the Philippine Republic, or why a country like India, which has just cut loose from its parent, often acts differently from a nation like France. They can see why a small nation like Switzerland plays a far different role in the world from that played by a large country like the Union of Soviet Socialist Republics, or why a poverty-stricken nation like India is concerned about different problems from those which disturb relatively rich countries like Sweden and the United States. They should learn, however, of the vast differences between people *within* any one nation.

Fourth, children should learn about the increasing interdependence of countries and peoples. From almost the beginning of a child's life in school, he can learn how nations and peoples depend upon each other. Whether it is from the games he plays, the music he sings, the foods he eats, or the devices and machines he uses, the elementary-school child can learn some extent of his debt to other peoples. This is one of the ways of developing an appreciation of other countries and peoples and our reliance on them, as well as their dependence upon us.

Carried a little further, this concept can lead boys and girls to see some of the problems which result from our "shrinking" world.

Fifth, children should learn that we need to communicate with people of other countries. Growing out of the concept of interdependence is the realization of the need for many kinds of communication. For younger children this may be illustrated best through the exchange with children of other lands of food, clothing, games, songs, and other items of interest to them. With older children this concept may be enlarged to include the exchange of ideas, the need for learning languages in order to communicate, and the importance of the air waves and the airways. Children need to act upon this idea as well as verbalize it. They may exchange drawings and letters with foreign children, earn money to assist the United Nations International Children's Emergency Fund, the Junior Red Cross, and other worthy international organizations, and in many ways actually communicate with peoples of other parts of the world. They may also take part in an active school affiliation service program (see Chapter 7, "Affiliations between Schools of Different Countries").

Last, children should learn that there are conflicts between countries, but that people in all parts of the world are trying to learn to live peacefully together in the world community. From the television screen and the radio, from the newsreel and the newspaper, from the conversation of older children and from adults, boys and girls are bound to hear about the international conflicts which plague the world. No realistic program of education for international understanding in the elementary school can ignore these conflicts. Without thrusting adult problems onto children, the story of conflicts can

22

be discussed simply and understandingly. At the same time, children need to know the story of man's efforts to achieve international cooperation. These may include accounts of the peaceful settlement of the dispute between Norway and Sweden, the cooperation of the United States and the U.S.S.R. in the cholera epidemic in Egypt, the work of the United Nations in helping victims of the earthquake in Ecuador, the work of the International Postal Union, and the peaceful maintenance of the undefended border between the United States and Canada. This is a part of the task of creating what Gordon Allport calls the "expectancy for peace." (M. Hadley Cantril, editor, *Tensions That Cause Wars*, 1950, ch. 2.)

DANGERS TO AVOID

In any program of study about other lands and peoples there are certain dangers which should be borne in mind and avoided. One is the tendency to stress the bizarre, the unique, the colorful, instead of the accurate, everyday, realistic features of a country. This is a special danger for the elementary school, where teachers are often looking for the colorful costumes and the strange customs which lend themselves to pageants and celebrations. Such an approach is exemplified by the stress on wooden shoes and windmills in the Netherlands, when wooden shoes are actually a rare sight there, and windmills are being preserved as museums because they are becoming as obsolete as our wooden covered bridges. Or such stress on the colorful may lead to false generalizations about Japan, which picture it in pre-World War II rather than in up-to-date scenes.

For some teachers there is the added danger of fostering uncritical good will. There are features of every country which are bad. They may be understood, but there is no reason to accept them as good or to attempt to explain them away.

A third danger is that of attempting to study too many countries, with the consequence that these studies turn into a cataloguing of factual information and a hodgepodge of learning. Similar to this is the attempt to cover every aspect of the life of a country rather than selecting aspects which can be meaningful to an elementary-school child.

Probably the most difficult danger to avoid is that of judging others by our own standards: If they have good modern plumbing and are Christians, they are civilized; if they wear few clothes or believe in passive resistance they are "backward"!

On all these points, it is the attitude of the teacher which will largely determine the approach to a country or culture. Perhaps the best way to start in any such program is for teachers themselves to probe their own prejudices about other countries and peoples!

CHARACTERISTICS OF A PROGRAM FOR THE ELEMENTARY SCHOOL

To be successful, any program of study of other lands and peoples must conform to the same criteria which exist for any other aim of the elementary school. These are well known to educators, but it may be important to review them briefly, with particular reference to learning about other countries and peoples.

Is Comprehensive. The study of other places and peoples should be an integral part of the elementary-school curriculum, intended for every child, but adapted to the differences in children according to locality, intelligence, reading ability, past experience, and interests. It should be a continuous and cumulative program, starting with the pre-school or primary school child learning to accept himself and to adjust to others, and continuing with his growth into an understanding of those who live farther away and who are different. It should be a balanced program, complementing the study of the local community and the United States, rather than replacing these important aspects of the elementary-school curriculum or crowding them into an obscure corner of the curriculum.

Provides a Variety of Experiences. So far as we now know, there is no *one* way of introducing children to other countries and peoples. Children need a variety of experiences. They need to meet people from other countries. They need to see films. They need to sing the songs and perform the dances of other peoples. They need to act out the fables and legends of other lands. They need to share experiences with the children of other lands—experiences which combine both emotional and intellectual approaches to foreign cultures.

Stresses Attitudes. Knowledge may be easily forgotten, and skills may disappear with lack of use, but attitudes usually cling to a person for life. All three are important, but the greatest is attitudes. That is where the stress should be in the presentation and evaluation of any program.

Leads to Action. Children learn what they live and do. This is a truism of education, but it is so often forgotten that I dare to mention it again. It is difficult to find realistic experiences involving action, but boys and girls should be engaged in some small project in connection with the study of another country, whether it be the preparation of a scrapbook about another land which will be sent to a children's hospital in this country, the drawing of pictures or the recording of songs of the United States which will be sent to a school abroad, the preparation of a mural or play which may be shown to other children, or the staging of a bazaar to raise funds to help some boy or girl in another land. From such activities children tend to retain more than from more passive types of learning.

Includes the Community. A child who learns at school to respect a Negro or Jew or Chinese is not likely to retain such an attitude if the home or community harbors prejudice against these groups. Such a situation has led social psychologists to emphasize the "total situation" approach to all kinds of learning, and has led educators to work much more closely with the home and community than they used to do. Difficult though it may be, the school which is really interested in a successful program of education about other countries and peoples *must* include parents and others in the local community in its program. Through mothers' meetings, parent-teacher associations, local libraries, churches, labor organizations, and other groups, the elementary school must cooperate with the adult community in any realistic program of this kind.

One of the most effective means of enlisting the cooperation of members of the adult community is to use them as resource persons in a school program on international understanding. Every school should certainly have a list of persons who have travelled recently abroad, of those who have lived abroad, and of those who have pictures and objects from abroad which they would be willing to show. Such persons, if willing, can be of great help in making other lands and peoples real to boys and girls, and in the process can themselves grow in their understanding of a school program. Likewise, some of the thousands of foreign students in the United States might be

26

used more effectively for educational purposes than we are now using them, if they were willing. Especially valuable would be the contribution of teachers from foreign countries.

Receives Active Support from the School's Administration. To be sure, something can be accomplished with the tacit approval of the administration, but much more can be done where there is active support. Time, equipment, and money are important for any program; without the enthusiastic approval of the administrators who usually provide these essentials, a program can be handicapped or even wrecked. Any program in the elementary school needs to involve the principal, the board of education, and the superintendent of schools.

Embodies Experimentation and Evaluation. Teachers have taught about other lands and peoples for many years, but they have had little proof that they really accomplished what they set out to do. They have taught as they were taught, and the vicious cycle has continued. Teachers today need to be aware of the latest scientific data on the formation and change of attitudes. (See pages 3-4 and 198.) They need to experiment with and evaluate new approaches. They need to jot down anecdotal records of children's comments during a study of another country. They need to experiment with stories written by boys and girls about children in another land before and after an intensive study of that country. They need to use social distance and attitude tests before a unit, at the close of a unit, and possibly six months after the unit is terminated. They need to appraise the films they have used and their temporary and long-term effects on children. They need to utilize the sociodrama. In such ways teachers can help in the important task of finding the most feasible ways of developing understanding and appreciation.

SELECTION OF COUNTRIES OR TOPICS TO BE STUDIED

There are over 70 countries, over 300 well-established cultures, and scores of topics dealing with various aspects of these countries and cultures, which vie for attention in our schools. How can one choose from such a wealth of possibilities the few on which to concentrate in the elementary school?

The Incidental Approach. The study of other parts of the world, particularly with younger children, may be largely incidental, introducing their stories, folk tales, songs, games, and celebrations into the general program of the elementary grades. Where there are children from other countries in the class, where visitors arouse an interest in another country, or where some special event creates curiosity, brief and simple studies can be made of ways of living in other lands. These studies will probably be infrequent.

The Topical Approach. In the intermediate grades there is much to be said for selecting topics which cut across national boundaries. Thus a study of food, clothing, transportation, communication, conservation, intercultural relations, or inventions might well start with the local community or the United States and lead the class to the study of these topics in another country. The study of food could well include a comparison of the wheat and corn culture of the United States with the rice culture of parts of China. The study of intercultural understanding could include a study of ways in which people of different backgrounds live in Brazil, Hawaii, or New Zea-

28

land. Or the study of inventions could demonstrate the contribution of inventors from many nations.

Small Countries with Relatively Simple Cultures. Another commendable approach in the elementary school seems to be the study of a few smaller countries with relatively simple cultures or with cultures similar to that of the United States. This would mean the study of one of the Scandinavian countries, the Netherlands, Switzerland, Australia or New Zealand, and possibly England. Children would thus be able to gain an understanding of some other countries without being plunged into the large and less easily understood cultures of China, India, or the U.S.S.R., for example.

Neighboring Nations. A study of Canada or Mexico has merit if well handled. Although not too simple to understand, they are still not completely foreign because of their proximity to the United States. There is the added advantage of the presence of people in almost any community who have been to one of these countries and can thus help children to understand these lands. And there is some possibility that boys and girls, with their parents, may be able to visit parts of these nations. These countries also loom fairly large in any study of the history of the United States and may be chosen for that reason.

Countries in which Pupils Are Particularly Interested. A school with an affiliated school abroad (see Chapter 7, "Affiliations between Schools of Different Countries") might well want to study that country in the elementary grades, despite the fact that it did not fit into any of the categories already listed. Likewise, a special interest growing out of an assembly program, a visit of a person from abroad, or a current happening might well turn the attention of a group of boys and girls to a particular nation. Sometimes the country from which their ancestors came to the United States has a special appeal. When such an interest has been aroused, it is usually important to capitalize upon it.

Countries against which Children Are Prejudiced. This approach, though neglected, has much merit and has frequently been employed in a few schools. If the children have developed a great deal of prejudice against a certain country, it would be well for the teacher to consider a study of that nation, particularly if there is a good chance of changing their attitudes through such study. Such a criterion has proved successful where teachers have presented their plans to the assembled parents of their pupils and have obtained their cooperation.

GENERAL METHODS OF TEACHING

There are many ways of approaching the study of other lands and peoples or of topics which involve other countries. Each teacher will need to select methods to suit his own teaching style and his particular group. However, teachers should bear in mind the findings of psychologists as to the methods most likely to result in better understanding of other lands and their inhabitants. These findings are presented in the next few pages in the order of their assumed value.

Teaching about Other Countries through Personal Contacts. Social psychologists are agreed that face to face contacts with persons of other races, religions, or nations, under favorable circumstances, are among the most valuable experiences in forming desirable attitudes. They seem to feel that such face to face experiences should be with one's peers and so far as possible in situations where all are on an equal basis socially.

Many educators interested in developing international un-

30

*Figure 3. Head of French school tells French tales to chil-
dren in American school during visit. Courtesy of Oak Lane
Country Day School, Philadelphia.*

derstanding are opposed to foreign travel for children, unless
they have the psychological security of travelling with their
families. Belgian educators take their elementary-school pupils
to France, where the language is the same and the culture
quite similar, but postpone till later any trips to countries with
different languages and sharper contrasts in culture. In the
United States, children seldom have the opportunity to visit
other countries, although the issue of the *National Education
Association Journal* for November, 1949, carries brief accounts
of fourth-grade children from the Laboratory School of the

Figure 4. A native Indian contributes to a study of India. Courtesy of Philadelphia Public Schools.

State Teachers College at Plattsburg, New York, taking a one-day trip with parents and teachers to Quebec, and pupils from the North Beach Elementary School in Miami, Florida, spending their Thanksgiving vacation in Cuba.

More schools make use of pupils of their own who have come from abroad, of parents or other adults in the community who have been born abroad or have lived there, or of foreign students studying in the United States, of whom there are nearly 30,000 at present. In her booklet on *World Understanding Begins with Children* (see bibliography at conclusion of chapter), Delia Goetz stresses the importance of and techniques for the preparation of children for the visits of persons from other countries.

Loretta Klee describes with great understanding the experiences of a second-grade class in an Ithaca, New York, school which planned an imaginary trip to Chile as a result of the enrollment of a Chilean boy in their class. (*Social Education*, April 1949, pp. 163-165.) Miss Klee has also vividly described the unpredictable results of a study of China and a visit of a Chinese student in a fourth grade, pointing out the advantages of first-hand contact as an essential part of a study of another nation. (*Social Education*, February, 1949, pp. 69-71.)

In the survey of Quaker schools described in the preface, the teachers expressed more interest in obtaining names of persons qualified to talk to children about other countries than in obtaining any other types of help. Schools would do well to keep lists of such resource people from among the students, teachers, parents, adults, and students from abroad in nearby colleges and universities.

Teaching about Other Countries through Audio-visual Experiences. Psychologists and educators, including those with considerable experience in the intercultural education movement, agree upon the importance of the audio-visual aids in attitude formation and change. As yet there are not too many good films or reliable and interesting filmstrips for use with boys and girls. Some teachers report effective use of the *Encyclopædia Britannica* films and filmstrips on *Children in Many Lands*. Some of these, however, are out of date and seem to stress the unusual rather than the usual. Elementary-school teachers generally seem pleased with the value of *Montevideo Family* (United World Films, 1943), and Walt Disney's *Grain That Built a Hemisphere* (Institute of Inter-American Affairs,

Figure 5. Visual aids help make a foreign land more real.
Courtesy of Keystone View Co., Meadville, Pennsylvania.

1943, on loan from some State Extension Division libraries), and the various titles of the United World Films on *The Earth and Its People*. The new series of filmstrips, *People Are People*, showing the lives of twelve families around the world, has also received enthusiastic endorsement.

A very valuable contribution could be made by a group of teachers in rating films and filmstrips about other countries as to their value for use in the elementary school. Meantime, teachers will need to rely on such listings as the *Educational Film Guide* and the *Filmstrip Guide*, which are located in most school and public libraries.

Studying Other Countries and Peoples

Teachers will find help in their search for pictures in a booklet by Bruce Miller (Ontario, California) on *Sources of Free and Inexpensive Pictures* and in *Units of Teaching Pictures* of the Informative Classroom Picture Publishers (Grand Rapids 2, Michigan).

Teaching about Other Countries through Creative Activities. The resourceful teacher will find many ways in which to involve pupils in creative activities in conjunction with their studies of other countries and peoples. Their value was apparent in a survey of high school seniors which the writer of this chapter made in fifteen schools across the United States (*Progressive Education*, May 1950). The only references they made to elementary-school experiences in arousing their interest in other parts of the world were in "projects," such as a pageant on China, a mural painted after a class had studied Sweden, a small classroom museum of Mexican objects started in connection with a study of that neighbor-nation, and a few similar activities. Herbert Read, using art in its broadest sense, stresses the importance of such creative activities, pointing out that "A child's art . . . is its passport to freedom." (*Education for Peace*, 1949, p. 152). With modern psychologists, he emphasizes the importance of creativity in channelling properly the aggressive tendencies of people.

Alert teachers will want to encourage their pupils to dramatize their readings, to create simple sociodramas, to paint murals, to make simple leather and woven goods, to collect stamps, to dress dolls in the costumes of other lands, to cook the foods of other nations, and to do various types of construction jobs. In this way they will begin to learn about other peoples through their hands as well as their heads.

35

Figure 6. Reproducing a Mexican market. Courtesy of Upper Darby (Pennsylvania) Public Schools.

Teaching about Other Countries through Reading. Reading about other countries has value, and no one of the approaches just discussed can be carried on adequately without it. However, reading activities are probably not as valuable in themselves as many teachers would like to believe. They need to be supplemented by some of the other experiences listed above. That is why reading is placed last on this brief list of methods, although stress is laid upon it as one aspect of a good program. The intercultural education movement has laid great stress on stories about children of other races and religions as a means of developing and changing attitudes, and it is probably true that stories about children in other lands can be made one of

36

Figure 7. Model of an Israeli kibbutz. Courtesy of Oak Lane Country Day School.

the most effective parts of a reading program in the elementary school when properly handled.

Fortunately, there is a growing list of authentic and interesting books for children, including stories, folk tales and legends, poetry, and novels. Good biographies and plays are less common. The bibliography which follows lists several children's books. For other titles, teachers can easily consult such standard references as *The Children's Catalogue* and May Hill Arbuthnot's *Children and Books*, 1947.

CONCLUSION

Helping children to understand and appreciate other countries and peoples is an immense task, but it can also be a thrilling adventure for both teachers and pupils. As a Chinese philosopher has said, "One of the measures of a man is his ability to live in the wide house of the world." Similarly, one of the measures of a teacher is his ability to help children to live in this "wide house of the world"—the world community. Such understanding and appreciation can begin in the elementary school through a many-sided program which is both exciting and profitable.

MATERIALS FOR TEACHERS AND PUPILS

Free and Inexpensive Materials
Free and Inexpensive Learning Materials. Nashville, Tennessee: George Peabody College, 1952. Includes some materials on world affairs.

Kenworthy, Leonard S. *Free and Inexpensive Materials on World Affairs.* Brooklyn College, Brooklyn, N. Y.: the Author, 1954. Includes many items for elementary schools.

Audio-visual Materials
Hartley, William H. *A Guide to Audio-Visual Materials for Elementary School Social Studies.* Brooklyn, N. Y. (50 Court Street): Rambler Press. Films, filmstrips, and slides listed and annotated.

Resource Units
See the *Education Index* for lists of units on various topics. Resource units may be purchased from the F. A. Owen Publishing Company, Dansville, N. Y., and the World Book Encyclopedia Reference Library, Merchandise Mart, Chicago, Illinois.

38

Children's Books on Other Lands and Peoples
Dratz, Eva M. *Aids to World Understanding: For Elementary School Children.* Minneapolis: Minneapolis Public Schools, 1950. 47 pp. Lists books for all member nations of the United Nations in 1949, with annotations on contents and reading level.

Kenworthy, Leonard S. *Asia in the Social Studies Curriculum* (includes materials on aims and lists of books, films, and filmstrips). *Developing World-Minded Children: Resources for Elementary School Teachers* (includes materials on topics and countries). *Studying France, Germany, Italy, and the Netherlands in Elementary Schools* (annotated lists of books, films, and filmstrips). *Studying the U.S.S.R.* (includes materials on aims and annotated lists of books, films, and filmstrips). Brooklyn College, Brooklyn, N. Y.: the Author. *Studying the U. N.* Brooklyn College, Brooklyn, N. Y.: the Author.

Series of Books for Boys and Girls
Holiday House: Lands and Peoples Series.

Knopf: Made in . . . Series.

Macmillan: Around the World Series.

Charles E. Merrill: World Geography Readers.

Messner: Adventure in . . . Series.

Row, Peterson: The Good Neighbor Series.

Bulletins for Teachers and Pupils
Air Age Education News. Air Age Education Research, 100 East 42nd Street, New York 17, N. Y.

American Junior Red Cross News. American Red Cross, 18th and D Streets, N. W., Washington 13, D. C.

Geographic School Bulletin. National Geographic Society, 16th and M Streets, N. W., Washington, D. C.

Guide to Parents and Teachers. American Friends Service Committee, 20 South 12th Street, Philadelphia 7, Penna.

Newsletter for Boys and Girls. American Friends Service Committee (see address in entry above).

Organizations for Special Materials
Foreign Policy Association, 22 East 38th Street, New York 16, N. Y.

National Geographic Society, 16th and M Streets, N. W., Washington, D. C.

Pan American Union, Washington 6, D. C.

United States Office of Education, Washington 25, D. C.

SUGGESTED READING

Association for Supervision and Curriculum Development. *Organizing the Elementary School for Living and Learning.* Washington, D. C.: National Education Association, 1947. Chapter 5, "Citizens of the World."

Dratz, Eva M. *Aids to World Understanding for Elementary School Children.* Minneapolis: Minneapolis Public Schools, 1950. Pamphlet.

————— *Guide to Teaching About the United Nations and World Affairs. A Teacher's Handbook.* Washington, D. C.: National Education Association, 1953. Pamphlet.

Goetz, Delia. *World Understanding Begins With Children.* Washington, D. C.: U. S. Office of Education, 1949. Pamphlet.

Kenworthy, Leonard S. *World Horizons for Children and Youth.* Brooklyn College, Brooklyn, N. Y.: the Author, 1952. Pamphlet.

Kohn, Clyde F., editor. *Geographic Approaches to Social Education.* Nineteenth Yearbook of the National Council for the Social Studies. Washington, D. C.: National Council for the Social Studies, 1948.

in the Elementary School

National Association of Elementary School Principals. *Learning Goodwill in the Elementary School.* Washington, D. C.: National Education Association, 1946.

Schell, Loretta Klee. "Developing International Understanding in the Elementary School." *Approaches to an Understanding of World Affairs.* Twenty-fifth Yearbook, National Council for the Social Studies. Washington, D. C.: National Council for the Social Studies, 1954, Chapter 16.

West, Edith, editor. *Improving the Teaching of World History.* Twentieth Yearbook of the National Council for the Social Studies. Washington, D. C.: National Council for the Social Studies, 1949.

3

Studying Other Countries and Peoples in the Secondary School

LEONARD S. KENWORTHY

High school youth today are the adults who will help decide and execute the domestic and foreign policies of the United States tomorrow. As citizens of the most powerful nation in the world they will help to decide whether the peoples of the underdeveloped areas of the world are to be exploited or assisted in achieving a better standard of living, whether world trade is to be stifled or strengthened, whether the white men of the world will live amicably or antagonistically as a minority with the other peoples of the earth, whether the United Nations is to be weakened or strengthened and world government eventually formed, and whether there is to be war or peace. They will help to create the climate of opinion which will make a world community possible or impossible. What a responsibility, and what an opportunity, for teachers in secondary schools today!

Figure 8. A visiting student from Iraq explains geography and conditions of his native land. Courtesy of George School, George School, Pennsylvania.

The Constitution of UNESCO declares that "Ignorance of each other's ways and lives has been a common cause, throughout the history of mankind, of that suspicion and mistrust between the peoples of the world through which their differences have all too often broken into war."

43

One of the chief tasks of the secondary school is to help to dispel such ignorance and to replace it with understanding and appreciation of other countries and peoples. This is a large and difficult assignment, but the peace of the world depends in part on the successful accomplishment of that task.

AIMS IN STUDYING OTHER COUNTRIES AND PEOPLES

There are many aims which teachers should bear in mind when guiding students in their study of other places and peoples. Each teacher will need to emphasize those points which seem important for the particular group with which he is working and with the particular subject which he is teaching. The following aims seem important:

To Understand and Appreciate the Likenesses and Differences between People and Why They Act as They Do. One of the main jobs of the secondary school is to help adolescents to understand themselves. Another is to help them to understand and to live peacefully with others, whether they be members of their own family, their friends, their classmates, their neighbors, or the peoples of their own and other countries. As President Roosevelt pointed out in the last speech he wrote before his death, "Today we are faced with the preeminent fact that, if civilization is to survive, we must cultivate the science of human relationships."

This means that teachers need to help students to understand the common interests of people everywhere, whether they are achieving status in a group, obtaining the minimum essentials of food, warmth, and shelter, expressing their creative abilities, or developing values or goals of living. (For a

44

fuller treatment of this idea see Stuart Chase, *The Proper Study of Mankind*, 1948, Chapter 8, "Common Patterns of Mankind.")

Teachers also need to help students to understand the differences which exist between people within a country and between the peoples of different countries, since peace is in large measure the adjustment of individuals and groups to differences. High-school students need to learn about the reasons for these differences and to adapt themselves so far as possible to such dissimilarities, realizing that the orchestration of personal and national differences is possible and desirable.

To Understand How Cultures Develop and Change. Adolescents can begin to understand the concept of culture, interpreting the word to mean "the whole integrated traditional body of ways of doing, thinking, and feeling that give a special group its character." (For a fuller treatment of this idea see Robert Redfield, "The Study of Culture in General Education," *Social Education* 11: 259-264; or Clyde Kluckhohn, *Mirror for Man*, 1949.) They can appreciate such factors as the effect of the physical environment, the country's folklore, religious beliefs, and institutions upon the way a country acts. They can recognize the variety of beliefs and ways of thinking or acting which exist within a country, whether it be India or Switzerland, Hawaii or Mexico. And they can grasp, in part at least, the central concept of *change*.

To Understand the Increasing Interdependence in the Modern World. Secondary-school students need to be acutely aware of the increasing interdependence in the modern world and the effect upon them of such interdependence. They need to develop an appreciation of their debt to other countries,

45

both in the past and in the present. Similarly, they need to realize some of the problems which result from increasing interdependence—problems of health, trade, travel, food, population pressures, governmental relations, and war and peace.

Of primary importance should be the students' realization that conflicts will continue to exist, but that war is not inevitable. In view of the results of the Purdue Poll of Young People (December, 1947, Division of Educational Reference, Purdue University, Lafayette, Indiana), which revealed a distressing view on the inevitability of war, this point needs particular emphasis. Teachers will probably find helpful such statements as the one by 2000 American psychologists on "Human Nature and the Peace" (see Sylvanus M. Duvall, *War and Human Nature*, New York: Public Affairs Committee, 1947), and the more recent statement by eight social scientists from six nations meeting under the aegis of UNESCO (see Hadley Cantril, editor, *Tensions That Cause Wars*, 1950).

To Understand the United States and Its World Relationships. The eminent anthropologist, Ralph Linton, emphasized an important truth when he declared that "Those who know no other culture than their own cannot know their own." One of the main reasons for studying other lands is to increase one's views of one's own country. Students need to know how many people of the world respect and admire the United States—and why. At the same time they need to know why there is a growing fear and distrust of the United States around the globe, whether it is because of our attitude toward the colored peoples of the world and our treatment of the Negro, our possession and use of the atom and hydrogen bombs and our tremendous military organization, our economic power, or our alleged hysteria and witch hunts of liberals, or whether other

46

factors are involved. From such knowledge should come a desire to change our national life to make it conform more nearly to our stated ideals, and the skills with which to bring about such changes.

To Understand Current World Affairs. Current events crowd into the life of every adolescent, and the school needs to help students to interpret the kaleidoscopic changes in the contemporary world. Part of the background for such an interpretation will come from the study of other lands and peoples, whether through a reading of their literature, a study of their history, or an understanding of their science, religions, or arts.

To Acquire Skill in Communication. Many students will never need to use a language other than English, but an increasing number of them will find the knowledge of a foreign language an important tool for living in the modern world. Taught with imagination and skill, the study of a foreign language can help students to understand other cultures and to communicate with them. At present there are far too few Americans who can communicate with peoples of other countries. As was pointed out in the preceding chapter, students also need to communicate in a variety of other ways, sharing with others through correspondence, exchange of gifts and ideas, and assistance to needy persons.

To Develop Specialization, Particularly along Vocational Lines. In the past the demand for persons who knew other countries and peoples was not great. With the increasing role which the United States is playing in the world, there are many more vocational opportunities in other countries which involve working with other people. Although this is primarily a responsibility of the colleges, vocational training at the high-school level can be a minor aim of studying other lands and peoples. And for those who do not expect to work abroad, there is an increasing need to know about other nations. The doctor, the scientist, the businessman, the teacher, the artist, and others need to keep informed of developments in their fields of specialty in other countries.

DANGERS AND DIFFICULTIES

Many of the dangers and difficulties mentioned in the previous chapter apply to the study of other lands and peoples in secondary schools, such as the danger of stress on the bizarre, uncritical good will, the superficial study of too many nations, and judgment of others by our own standards. In addition, there seem to be two difficulties which are peculiar to secondary schools.

One is the difficulty of segmentation. To study a country or culture adequately involves seeing that nation or culture as a whole, including its environment, its ways of making a living, its techniques, its institutions, its methods of discovery and invention, its concepts of group welfare, its beliefs and traditions. If social studies teachers try to do all this under the present departmental organization, they will be swamped. If each separate subject field tries to cover certain aspects of a country, the result is compartmentalization or neglect of some aspects of that country or culture. The only adequate answer seems to be the adoption of a well-integrated program or of some type of area studies.

Another difficulty is that of examinations. Even though there has been some modification in college entrance examinations and state examinations, the existence of these, plus department or city exams, still militates against the kind of program which is being outlined here. For example, a teacher of the social studies might want to spend several days on a study of modern Germany or Italy, bringing the story of those countries up to date, rather than merely touching on the rise of fascism under Hitler and Mussolini just because it is so developed in the text. Too often the teacher is discouraged from doing this by heads of departments or by principals who fear that the pupils will not do well on city or state examinations. Part of the answer to this problem lies in the continual improvement of such tests. Meanwhile, most teachers could probably go a long way in extending their treatment of foreign cultures without impairing their students' performance on standardized tests.

CHARACTERISTICS OF A PROGRAM FOR SECONDARY SCHOOLS

In planning a program of study about other countries and peoples in the secondary schools, several points should be kept in mind. These principles of curriculum construction apply as much to such a program as we are outlining here as to other aspects of the total school program. Among the most important of these principles are the following:

Permeating every Subject Field. Where it is impossible to develop a core course or integrated program, persons responsible for a program in international civic education should see to it that the study of other lands and peoples becomes an integral part of every subject field. Teachers of the social studies may bear the major responsibility, but the teachers of literature can contribute much through the study of novels, plays, poetry, biography, and other writings of other nations. Science teachers can include the contribution of persons from

49

many lands to the world's storehouse of knowledge by holding discussions of race problems, problems of food and health, data on atomic energy, biographies of famous scientists, and the work of the Food and Agriculture Organization and the World Health Organization. Teachers of art and music can also contribute much, especially through emotionalized experiences, to the adolescent's understanding of other peoples, of their reaction to their environment and beliefs, their contributions to world culture, and their dependence upon still other peoples in art forms. In fact, every subject can make some contribution to the aim of developing understanding, respect, and admiration for the peoples of the whole world.

To achieve the best results in a school-wide program requires some kind of coordination. One way to do this is to have a committee on world affairs made up of members from different departments, not forgetting the teachers of science, art, music, home economics, and the manual arts. A less desirable but more practical suggestion is to place the responsibility for coordination in the hands of the curriculum coordinator or the person who performs that major function.

Utilizing Co-curricular Activities. Assemblies, language clubs, international or world affairs clubs; school plays; the celebration of special events such as Pan-American Day, United Nations Week, World Brotherhood Day, book fairs, film showings at lunch periods, and other co-curricular activities should loom large in any school program on other countries. From what is known about attitude formation and change, these activities may be the most significant parts of any attempt to develop an interest in and understanding of our world neighbors.

If a student carries on a correspondence with a student

abroad, takes part in a panel or debate before a local civic organization, participates in a public opinion poll, or entertains a student from abroad, he is much more likely to develop worthwhile attitudes on world affairs than if his experience in this field is limited to reading a book about other lands or peoples.

Integration with the Elementary School Program. It should be assumed that any program in the junior and senior high schools would be built upon the program of the elementary school, but practice is so often to the contrary that it is worth emphasizing at this point. Cumulative records of what groups of students have studied, of attitude tests, of special activities undertaken, and of student reactions should be sent to the junior high school from the elementary school and to the senior high school from the junior high school. There should be some communication and common planning among the teachers of these various units.

Integration with Studies of the Local Community and Nation. Programs in intercultural and international education can be so closely related that they should be carefully integrated. For example, the study of Italy or Denmark should include the story of the migrations of Italians or Danes, as the case may be, to the United States and the problems which ensued, as well as the contributions of either immigrant group to life in the United States. The study of minority problems or transient populations in the United States should lead to a study of these problems on a world scale. Every opportunity should be utilized to integrate studies of the local community, nation, and world.

Stressing Attitudes and Action. The tendency of the junior and senior high schools is to stress factual information to the neglect of attitudes and action. A realistic program for these educational levels should be acutely aware of this fact and make every effort to emphasize attitudes and involve students in activities relating to other lands and peoples, such as are described in Chapters 4 to 8 of this book.

Capitalizing upon Adolescent Interests. Because of the adolescent's desire to become a part of the adult world, high-school students should occasionally participate in activities with adults, whether these be attendance at a Foreign Policy Luncheon, a local forum on world affairs, or a community-wide campaign for CARE packages to be sent abroad. Older adolescents should be encouraged to join groups with adult members, such as the American Association for the United Nations, the Foreign Policy Association, and the United World Federalists.

Adolescents are interested in social activities; therefore, experiences such as dances, picnics, hikes, boat trips, or hay rides with students from abroad should be encouraged.

The fact that adolescents often desire to be active and practical should lead to stress on projects which appeal to this characteristic, such as week-end work camps (see Chapter 8) with students of other races and religions, sending of books and clothing abroad, and assistance to newcomers from abroad in the local community.

Providing a Variety of Experiences. Because of the variety of students in secondary schools and their increasingly specialized interests, any secondary-school program should provide a rich assortment of approaches. Contacts with peers and adults from abroad will probably be the most effective type of experience, followed closely by films on other countries and peoples, music and art, map-making, foreign correspondence,

52

Figure 9. Map-making is one road to world understanding.

dramatics, and service projects. (For data on student interests, see Leonard S. Kenworthy, "High School Seniors and World-Mindedness," *Progressive Education*, May, 1950, pp. 205-207.)

Involving the Adult Community. It is just as important to utilize the resources of the entire community and to involve

53

adults in a secondary-school program as in an elementary-school program, although often more difficult. Students can present panels, sponsor film showings, conduct polls of public opinion, and in other ways work with adults. Moreover, parents and other adults can be used in classes, clubs, and assemblies.

Including Adequate Coordination. Because of the departmentalization of most secondary schools, the problem of coordination looms larger at this level than in the elementary school. As was mentioned previously, a committee, preferably of elementary- and secondary-school teachers and wherever possible of students and parents, should be responsible for the stimulation and coordination of all aspects of the school's program in international civic education. Often this same group will be responsible for the local and national civic education programs as well.

Embodying Experimentation and Evaluation. Wherever possible, individual teachers, departments, or if possible, entire schools or school systems, should engage in experimentation on methods and materials for studying other countries and peoples. Whether students become interested in other parts of the world better by area studies (that is, the systematic study of some natural area of the world such as Scandinavia, the Near East, or Latin America), by co-curricular activities, or by regular subject courses needs to be investigated. Evaluation of films by students needs to be carried on. Tests of attitudes need to be developed. The influence of teachers as opposed to that of parents could well stand investigation. These and a host of other topics call for experimentation and evaluation. (For an account of one such investigation see Loretta Klee, "How Do You Feel About World Peace? A Study of Some Changes

54

in Expressed Attitudes of Senior High School Students,"
Journal of Educational Research, November, 1949, pp. 189-196.)

CHOOSING THE TOPICS OR COUNTRIES TO BE STUDIED

Teachers may find difficulty in determining which of the many countries and cultures of the world they will select for study. The growing tendency to permit more freedom of choice rather than dictating what must be studied makes some criteria of selection very important. The following bases of choice are therefore suggested:

Countries which Illustrate a Topic. Choice of countries to be studied is often dictated by the topic or topics being studied. Thus, a social studies class studying planning might want to investigate what has been done in the U.S.S.R., in Sweden, in the Netherlands, and in Puerto Rico in various aspects of governmental and private planning. A class in literature considering poetry might well choose selections from the poetry of China and India, the U.S.S.R., Chile, and two or three western European nations. A group learning about symphony orchestras could very profitably study the outstanding achievements of the orchestras of Prague, Vienna, Berlin, Paris, Amsterdam, and London, as well as several in the United States. And an art class studying art as an expression of a people's ways of living might choose such contrasting cultures as China, Haiti, Norway, and Mexico to illustrate its point.

Countries Representing Cultures. In the social studies, literature, art, and music, one of the best methods of selection is to choose a few nations which represent distinct cultures. Thus in art, there might well be a study of Oriental art, Latin-Amer-

55

ican art, Russian art, and Scandinavian art, while in literature a similar series of units might be set up. In addition to the intrinsic worth of this method there are the added advantages of possible correlation with area studies in the social studies and the fact that several art histories and anthologies of world literature are written according to such a plan.

The "Great Powers" and Countries which Are Increasingly Important. Certainly no student should graduate from high school without having studied something about the Great Powers—England, China, France, the U.S.S.R., and the United States. Since these are large countries with fairly complicated cultures, the study of them should be postponed at least until the junior high-school period. In addition to them, there is much to be said of a study of certain countries which are increasingly important, such as Brazil, Canada, and India, and at least one country from the Near East, possibly Turkey.

Countries in which Students Have a Particular Interest. Current world happenings, a school affiliation (see Chapter 7, "Affiliations between Schools of Different Countries"), an exhibit or program in the school or community, the visit of a person from abroad, a movie, or some other experience may make the study of a particular country especially interesting to students. Teachers would do well to capitalize upon such an interest so far as that is possible within the framework of the school's program.

Countries about which There Is the Most Prejudice or the Least Knowledge. Observations by teachers or objective tests may reveal a great deal of prejudice and/or a scant knowledge about a nation. In such a case that particular country might well be worth a special study by one or more departments of the school. A study of Russian, Brazilian, or Mexican music or art might do a great deal to overcome a feeling that these people are "inferior." The study of the transformation of large areas of wasteland in Israel, of the river valley projects in India or China, or hydro-electric plants in Africa might do considerable good in overcoming the feeling that these peoples are "backward." Particular attention is called to the prevailing ignorance of the citizens of the United States on the Far East, the Near East, Africa, and Southeast Asia as areas of the world worthy of special attention.

GENERAL METHODS AND MATERIALS FOR SECONDARY SCHOOL STUDENTS

From what is now known about effective teaching about other lands and peoples, a program in the secondary schools should probably concentrate on four approaches: providing contacts with persons from abroad, arranging audio-visual experiences, encouraging creative activities, and providing reading of various kinds to serve as a background for all these other experiences. Within each of these four approaches, we shall attempt to suggest certain tried and proved experiences.

Personal Contact with Persons from Other Countries. A few schools have been able to arrange for small groups of their students to learn about other countries and peoples from first-hand contact abroad. The George School in Bucks County, Pennsylvania, has had work camps in Germany during the past several summers and Germantown Friends School has had similar programs over a shorter period. Friends Central School in Philadelphia has a Student Abroad Plan whereby four students in their junior year study in Mexico and live in private homes there. The Verde Valley School in Sedona, Arizona, takes a camping trip to Mexico each spring. Student

57

groups from the Putney School in Putney, Vermont, and the Ethical Culture Schools in New York City have also gone abroad. The students of the Charlotte High School in Rochester, New York, have an annual exchange of visits with the Northern Vocational School of Toronto, Canada. All of these schools but one are private schools.

A few mature high-school students can be encouraged to travel or work abroad, going over with such organizations as the Experiment in International Living (Putney, Vermont), or the Youth Hostel Association (Northfield, Massachusetts), but for a large majority of students this is still a very expensive proposition. (For details on several such groups, see the booklet *Study, Travel, Work Abroad*, United States Student Association, Madison 5, Wisconsin.)

Schools, however, can arrange for their students to visit the International Houses which are established in large cities. They can invite students from abroad for weekend entertainment or to school functions. They can arrange for the visit of foreign high-school students who are visiting in this country for such events as the New York Herald-Tribune Youth Forum, Boy and Girl Scout Jamborees, or special visits such as have been carried on by the citizens of Nashville, Tennessee, and Wayne, Pennsylvania. In addition, there are often students and parents in the community with special knowledge of foreign countries who can be called upon to share their knowledge.

Audio-visual Experiences. There is now a wealth of excellent films and film-strips suitable for use in secondary-school classes, clubs, assemblies, lunch period film showings, and other ways. These can provide fairly satisfactory vicarious experiences in contacting people from other lands and learning about their ways of living, their institutions, their vocations, and other phases of their countries. Listings of visual aids appear in the *Educational Film Guide* and the *Filmstrip Guide*, which are located in most libraries. Also helpful is the National Education Association's *International Understanding: Catalogue of 16mm. Films*, 1950. Among the films which students and teachers have rated high are the Julien Bryan and United World Films, *Dragon Seed, Farrebique* (the story of French rural life), *Man to Man to Man, Dunant of the Red Cross, Open City, Paisan, Shoe Shine, Symphonie Pastorale*, and *Wilson*. Several of these have been shown in local theaters and have made a deep impression on high-school students.

Students can also gain much from trips to museums, art galleries, and theaters showing foreign films. Exhibits and bulletin boards by and/or for students in the school library, school corridors, classrooms, or in strategic places in the community, can be stimulating and educational.

Students should also have some opportunity during their high-school years to study the various radio and television news broadcasts and programs on world affairs and their objectivity and value. Some of the recordings of programs from the *Cavalcade of America, Americans All—Immigrants All*, and *You Were There* are important teaching devices. Recordings of the voices of people, such as the albums, *I Can Hear It Now* and the *Spiritual Message* by Gandhi, add an air of reality to the study of other lands and peoples. (For other valuable records see Gertrude B. Broderick, *Recordings for School Use: A Catalogue of Appraisals*. Chicago: Association for Education by Radio, 228 LaSalle Street.)

Creative Activities. Any program for learning about other countries and peoples, like any other educational program, should involve much learning by doing. There are many such

59

possibilities, and teachers and students will be able to add many more to the list which follows.

It is difficult and sometimes dangerous to differentiate between junior and senior high-school activities, but making scrapbooks, drawing pictures, making Christmas cards, dressing dolls, making toys, and collecting sports equipment and clothing seem to have particular appeal for junior high-school students. This group may be interested in foreign correspondence, too, and in dramatics. Senior high-school students can do research and report on it; participate in panels and debates in classes, in assemblies, and in the community; prepare and give radio programs; sponsor international dances; aid immigrant families or displaced persons; make polls of public opinion; take trips to the United Nations headquarters or to International Houses in nearby cities; teach classes in English to immigrants; collect books, clothes, and other materials to be sent abroad; and organize student clubs on world affairs.

Many schools try to involve the entire school in some one project, often making this an annual affair. In some cases it will be a school affiliation with a school abroad (see Chapter 7, "Affiliations between Schools of Different Countries."). In other cases it may be a pageant or model assembly of the United Nations or one of its specialized agencies (material available from the American Association for the United Nations, 45 East 65th Street, New York 21, N. Y.); and in still other cases an annual contest to select a world-minded person whose picture will be hung in the Hall of World Heroes or Hall of World Citizens.

Midwood High School in Brooklyn, New York, has such a contest annually, participated in by the entire school, with one outstanding person selected by the vote of the school each

Figure 10. A student reports on his research.

year. Two recent choices have been Ralph Bunche and Albert Schweitzer. (For other possible nominees see Leonard S. Kenworthy's *Twelve Citizens of the World*, 1953.)

Reading. Undergirding all these activities and permeating every subject field should be a rich reading program, stimulated by the teachers, by students, by the school librarian, and by the local librarians. Such reading should include a daily newspaper and the reading of occasional magazine articles, with teachers, librarians, and students calling the attention of students to articles of interest and importance. It should also include novels about other countries, biographies, plays, poetry, and informational books. Often these will be chosen

61

on the basis of vocational interests. The teachers of every subject field have a responsibility for such a reading program, but
the teachers of literature, social studies, and foreign languages
have special opportunities along these lines. Sir Richard Living-
stone has referred to literature as "a railway ticket, costing
very little, that takes men to every country in the world, a pass
that admits to the greatest of waxwork exhibitions, where
every waxwork is made of flesh and blood." (*The Future in
Education*, 1945, p. 80.) The trouble with most of our reading
programs in the high school is that the railroad tickets have
been too exclusively for local commuting trains; some of them
should be turned in for passage on modern transcontinental
airplanes. When teachers think in terms of what type of reading to encourage, they would do well to think in terms of the
twentieth-century world.

These and other methods not mentioned in this chapter are
merely means to achieve the desirable ends outlined on pages
44-48. The value of any activity depends upon the degree to
which it helps achieve these major objectives. Many ways will
be found of ascertaining whether these objectives have been
achieved. Among them will be the use of attitude tests before
and after the study of a country or culture, anecdotal reports
based on comments of pupils, observation of skills used during
the study, behavior when entertaining visitors to the class from
the countries being studied, and application of knowledge to
interpretation of current events. Teachers will want to evaluate attitudes, skills, and knowledge—probably in that order of
importance.

CONCLUSION

People sometimes speak of the shrinking world of today. That is true in some ways. But as it shrinks, teachers need to help their students to understand and appreciate far more of it than was previously necessary. In terms of former learning requirements, therefore, we live in an expanding world, and it is to such a world that secondary-school teachers need to orient their students. Only if teachers themselves are appreciative of other countries and peoples can they expect to develop such attitudes in their students, since these attitudes are caught more often than they are taught. Thus, the teachers of secondary schools in the United States have a tremendous responsibility and opportunity to serve as informed interpreters to youth of the global society in which we all live in this second half of the twentieth century.

MATERIALS FOR TEACHERS AND STUDENTS

General Methods and Materials—Booklets

Kenworthy, Leonard S. *Asia in the Social Studies Curriculum.* Brooklyn College, Brooklyn, N. Y.: The Author, 1951. Includes material on aims and lists of books, films, and filmstrips by countries.

———— *Free and Inexpensive Materials on World Affairs.* Brooklyn College, Brooklyn, N. Y.: The Author, 1954. Includes materials on world problems and countries.

———— *Studying the U.S.S.R.* Brooklyn College, Brooklyn, N. Y.: The Author, 1953. Includes material on aims and lists of books, films, and filmstrips.

———— *Studying the U. N.* Brooklyn College, Brooklyn, N. Y.: The Author, 1953.

UNESCO. *Towards World Understanding.* New York: Columbia University Press. A series of booklets. Of special value in studying other lands and peoples are the two on *The Teaching of Geography* and *The Teaching of History.*

Series of Books for High-School Students
(See also *Series of Books for Boys and Girls* at end of Chapter 2.)
Lippincott: Portraits of Nations Series.
Row, Peterson: World Neighbor Series. (Especially on Latin America.)

Anthologies for English Classes
Hoffman, David M. *Let's Get Acquainted: Readings for Understanding the Democratic Peoples of the World.* New York: Harper, 1948.

James, Thelma G., Walter R. Northcutt, and Marquis E. Shattuck. *World Neighbors.* New York: Harper, 1950.

Stovall, Floyd, Leo Hughes, and Haldeen Braddy. *Reading Around the World.* New York: Macmillan, 1947.

Van Doren, Carl. *Anthology of World Prose.* New York: Reynal, 1935.

Yutang, Lin. *The Wisdom of China and Asia.* New York: Random House, 1942.

Organizations Interested in World Affairs
American Association for the United Nations, 45 East 65th Street, New York, N. Y.

American Friends Service Committee, 20 South 12th Street, Philadelphia 7, Pennsylvania.

Foreign Policy Association, 22 East 38th Street, New York 16, N. Y.

National Education Association, Committee on International Relations, 1201 16th Street, Washington, D. C.

Pan American Union, Washington 6, D. C.

in the Secondary School

U. S. National Commission for UNESCO, Department of State, Washington 25, D. C.

U. S. Office of Education, Washington 25, D. C.

SUGGESTED READING

Arndt, Christian O., and Samuel Everett, editors. *Education for a World Society.* Eleventh Yearbook of the John Dewey Society. New York: Harper, 1951.

Committee on International Relations of the National Education Association, the Association for Supervision and Curriculum Development, and the National Council for the Social Studies. *Education for International Understanding in American Schools: Suggestions and Recommendations.* Washington, D. C.: National Education Association, 1948.

Haefner, John H. "Developing International Understanding in the Secondary School." *Approaches to an Understanding of World Affairs.* Twenty-fifth Yearbook of the National Council for the Social Studies. Washington, D. C.: National Council for the Social Studies. Chapter 17.

Kenworthy, Leonard S. *Twelve Citizens of the World.* New York: Doubleday, 1953.
——— *World Horizons for Children and Youth.* Brooklyn College, Brooklyn, N. Y.: The Author, 1952. Pamphlet.

——— *World Horizons for Teachers.* New York: Bureau of Publications, Teachers College, Columbia University, 1952.

Kohn, Clyde F., editor. *Geographic Approaches to Social Education.* Nineteenth Yearbook of the National Council for the Social Studies. Washington, D. C.: National Council for the Social Studies, 1948.

Matthews, Robert J. *Language and Area Studies in the Armed Forces: Their Future Significance.* Washington, D. C.: American Council on Education, 1947.

West, Edith, editor. *Improving the Teaching of World History.* Twentieth Yearbook of the National Council for the Social Studies. Washington, D. C.: National Council for the Social Studies, 1949.

4

Service Activities

MARY ESTHER MC WHIRTER

Service activities provide children with a practical approach to understanding foreign peoples—an approach which tends to be more gripping and to bite deeper than sheer academic study. The first part of this chapter will consider service activities at the elementary-school level and the chapter will conclude with a discussion of how they operate at the secondary-school level.

SERVICE ACTIVITIES IN ELEMENTARY SCHOOLS

"What do you think about sending these?" asks a sixth-grade teacher in a West Virginia town. As she raises the question, she holds up a pair of dirty pink bedroom slippers trimmed with what once had been white fur. A number of children look doubtful, but Jack, usually the spokesman for the class, declares, "Sure, those shoes are all right to send. If the people over there haven't got shoes they ought to be mighty glad for 'most anything we send 'em."

A week passes. Each day the sixth graders bring in more and more shoes. As they do so, they work out their own standards for judging each pair:

67

*Figure 11. Christmas packages ready for children abroad.
Courtesy of Oak Lane Country Day School, Philadelphia.*

"Will these shoes keep someone's feet warm and dry?"

"Would *I* like to receive these shoes?"

"Are these shoes good enough for a friendship-gift?"

With growing concern and interest they look at photographs of shoe-less boys and girls as well as at photographs of those made happy by gifts of American footwear. Stories also help to make these needy, far-away friends seem like real people, not just "the poor."

Role playing enables the sixth graders further to identify themselves with the boys and girls who will receive the shoes. Timmy, imagining himself a child in a German refugee camp, tries on a pair of sturdy shoes. "These fit me. They have thick soles. They will keep my feet warm. I like them."

Slowly, imperceptibly, there are changes in the children's

68

Figure 12. Streamers from tables to map show to which countries packages will go. Courtesy of Oak Lane Country Day School, Philadelphia.

thinking about the recipients. As the days go by, the differences between "them" and "us" grow smaller as more and more *likenesses* are discovered.

Then, on the last day of the shoe drive, Ginny contributes a pair of slightly worn oxfords which she herself has outgrown. Looking them over with a critical eye, Jack remarks, "See, there's a little rip on the side of this shoe. We can't send it like this. The kid over there who got it would get her feet wet when it rained or snowed. We ought to take some money from our class treasury and get the shoemaker to sew this up."

And this boy speaking is the same Jack of just a week ago!

69

Well, no, not quite the same Jack. It is probable that he will never again be the same Jack because now he has begun to have an inkling of what it means, literally, to "stand in someone else's shoes."

In a rural school in southern California a group of children cluster around an exhibit of paintings. Their attention is riveted upon a Japanese picture which shows a family harvesting rice. There is much talk about farming—a subject familiar to all the children.

"What do *your* fathers need as they farm *their* land?" asks the teacher.

Quickly the children answer, "Rich soil ... good seed ... sun ... rain ..."

Then, "Why?" queries the teacher.

"So they will get a big crop."

"And why do they want a big crop?"

"So as to have something to sell and something to feed their families."

Then, back to the Japanese painting. "Does this farmer have any of the same needs as he tills *his* field?"

Next, the children face the question, "What kind of a crop does the Japanese farmer hope to have? Why?"

And so, through a painting from the brush of an eleven-year-old Japanese school child, these American pupils discover some of the basic human needs which are universal.

A transparency portraying the Nativity story is placed in the window sill. As the sun shines through the rich colors of the tissue paper, the children gasp with surprise and delight.

"It's beautiful!"

"And what *careful* work!" So comments Joey who has a reputation for slap-dash art work, besmeared with paste.

"Who made it?" ask several children, their eyes still upon the transparency.

"This is the gift of a ten-year-old German child." The teacher's reply is amazing to her pupils.

"We couldn't do half so good."

"I'll say not."

"They sure can do better pictures than us."

Incorrect grammar is ignored as the teacher silently rejoices because of these newly-emerging attitudes of appreciation and humility shown by her sometimes arrogant fourth-graders.

As they continue to enjoy the picture, German Christmas customs which have become dear to American hearts are recalled. On this bright May morning, the singing of *Silent Night* takes on new meaning as the young singers realize, for the first time, that this hymn, like the transparency in the window before them, is a gift *to* us *from* Germany. That people in other countries make rich contributions to American life is a brand new idea for these fourth-graders. "Getting used to that idea will take time," ruminates the teacher as the last notes of the Christmas carol die away.

These two thumb-nail sketches, drawn from real life, are not unique. On the contrary, they epitomize the kinds of experiences which thousands of children are having as they cooperate in the work of organizations such as the American Friends Service Committee, CARE, Church World Service, Junior Red Cross, UNESCO, Save the Children Federation, and the Women's International League for Peace and Freedom—to mention but a few. Teachers in elementary schools value such experiences as means whereby their pupils are often led to realize that all people are members of God's family and there-

71

Figure 13. Sharing with neighbors overseas through Junior Red Cross. Courtesy of Grand Rapids (Michigan) Public Schools and the American Junior Red Cross News.

fore brothers and sisters; appreciate the differences, as well as similarities, which exist between people of varying races, nationalities, and cultures; and find joy in sharing across economic, racial, and national lines not only material goods, but also ideas, skills, and traditions.

Sharing Projects for Children. As will be noted, the word "sharing" rather than "giving" is used. Generally speaking, agencies dedicated to international understanding prefer the term "sharing" because it connotes a sense of responsibility on the part of the giver; a respect for the recipient; and a gracious acceptance of any gifts received *from* him. Later in this chapter more will be said about gifts sent from abroad to American children.

At the present time, numerous sharing projects for children are being carried forward by many agencies—a few of which are listed at the close of this chapter. Before launching any project it is well to secure current, accurate, and detailed information by writing directly to the agency with which you plan to work.

In thinking about service activities, teachers immediately ask, "What kinds have real meaning for children?" Experience has shown that there are three types to which children respond with high enthusiasm. In connection with each type, illustrations given here are largely in terms of American Friends Service Committee projects. These were chosen merely because they are well known to the writer of this chapter, and because she has had frequent opportunities to gather first-hand data concerning them.

1. *Children gather gifts-in-kind*

It's Hallowe'en: Friendly Beggars' Night. The children go out begging, yes! But this time their begging takes a new twist. Instead of collecting candy, cookies, and apples for themselves, the young beggars gather soap, sewing materials, and children's clothing to ship abroad. Each year at Hallowe'en time American children gather *tons* of such goods. This is not an exaggeration, but a report of actual warehouse weighing. Conservatively estimated, the valuation runs over the $25,000 figure. But that is the least important part of the story. The deeper values can never be weighed or measured because they are in the hearts and minds of the youngsters who participate in this enterprise.

How do these youngsters react? Let us listen to reports from teachers.

In a letter dated *February 7th* (and we do mean February!), an Ohio teacher declared: "Enthusiasm for the Hallowe'en project still runs high! One sixth-grade boy, very skeptical about the whole thing before it started, objected by saying, 'Aw, that won't be any fun. You can't soap windows, or do nothin'.'

"On Hallowe'en night he returned from his rounds as a Friendly Beggar, bringing in a heaped-up collection bag that, when emptied, filled two boxes. With a sheepish grin he commented, 'Remember how I told you it wouldn't be any fun? Well, I was wrong. It was fun!' Then he added, 'I never before had such a good time on Hallowe'en. The people who gave me this stuff were so nice. This year nobody yelled at us.'"

A Vermont teacher found children equally responsive to the opportunity to celebrate Hallowe'en in this new, constructive way. This is what her letter said: "We are again planning to carry out the project for Hallowe'en. I hadn't said anything about it, but the other day several of the children who had taken part in last year's observance came to me and asked if they could '*please* do it again this year'—that is, be Friendly Beggars. I agreed. Then the rest all wanted to join. I am thrilled by their response."

A Scout leader wrote: "Members of Troop No. 4 enjoyed immensely their Hallowe'en project. They made posters for store windows, wrote notices for the local paper, and constructed orange paper Hallowe'en pumpkins for door tags—

74

all in preparation for this trick-or-treat sortie. The public seemed to enjoy the idea as well as the children, since the response was so unprecedented. The girls are now looking forward to trimming a Mitten Tree."

These three messages, chosen at random from the correspondence files, can be duplicated many times over. Hundreds of leaders, like those quoted, indicated that as children were Friendly Beggars, they found joy in doing something constructive rather than destructive on Hallowe'en; were glad for the opportunity to help meet real needs of real people; felt satisfaction as they cooperated with adults of good will in their own communities; had opportunity for creative expression through drawing and writing; and wished to repeat the same service project and/or choose another one in the immediate future.

LET'S FILL A *Check-po* FOR A CHILD IN KOREA. Small hands were busy with the task of hemming large squares of sturdy cloth. With painstaking care these same small hands added feather-stitch trimmings in order to "brighten up" the book cloth or *check-po*, as a Korean child would call it. Each *check-po* was filled with school supplies essential the world around: writing tablets, pencils, erasers, crayons, drawing paper, small pencil sharpeners, and a few extras such as compasses and protractors. When the collection of materials was completed and arranged in a neat pile, the four ends of the cloth were tied together in kitty-corner fashion. Then a *check-po* was ready for its long journey to Korea, where it was proudly carried to school by its young recipient.

CLOTHES AND SEWING MATERIALS. Gathering these practical items for shipment abroad has been an exciting enterprise for many children in this country. Again and again their teachers

75

have displayed fine skill in linking this service activity to various subjects: to geography as the children located on maps the countries to which the gifts would be sent; to arithmetic as young mathematicians counted, weighed, and measured the goods; to art as they made drawings, posters, and signs to help in collecting these gifts-in-kind; to music as the youngsters learned folk songs of the lands where the clothing and sewing materials would be received; and to creative writing as the children composed stories, plays, and poems reflecting feelings of friendship toward the unknown, far-away boys and girls who later received the gifts.

In summary, this should be said: Leaders in most service agencies agree that projects which involve children in the gathering of gifts-in-kind are intended only incidentally for the purpose of collecting material goods, even though these are desperately needed. Leaders believe that the basic purpose behind such service activities is to help boys and girls grow in understanding and appreciation of other members of the human family and in the desire to share with these faraway people.

2. *Children make gifts*

LET'S TRIM THE MITTEN TREE. "Yes, *let's* trim the Mitten Tree!" This has been the eager response voiced by school children from Maine to California, from the Canadian line to the Mexican border. With painstaking care they have crocheted, knitted, and sewed mittens. What pride and satisfaction have been theirs as they contemplated the results of their labors: a Christmas tree laden with warm, bright, beautiful mittens for children abroad who know only want and poverty in their war-torn homelands.

76

Figure 14. Trimming a mitten tree. Courtesy of Rochester (N.Y.) Times-Union.

Quite frequently the young donor has slipped into his pair of gift-mittens a small card bearing his name and address. In some cases this has resulted in an exchange of letters.

What has this service activity meant to the participants? Let us read a few unsolicited letters from the files.

From a Pennsylvania teacher: "The children were delighted with their beautiful Mitten Tree and had a happier-than-usual Christmas because they shared and made *others* happy." And then, in another paragraph: "We made posters, wrote songs, stories, and poems about our Mitten Tree. We had fun trimming it. It was as high as the ceiling. A number of children brought flash cameras and took pictures of it. The sixth-grade girls knit mittens. Our school principal, several teachers, our ministers, parents, and other adult friends all came to see our Tree. We want to do another project next year."

"Jersey City" was the postmark on the envelope containing this next letter. "The mittens that we are sending were hung on our tree by second-grade children. They enjoyed thinking about the boys and girls who would be wearing the mittens that they brought."

From still another letter: "The weather here in Texas has been anything but cold. Nevertheless, our pupils entered into the spirit of the Mitten Tree project. It was a far greater pleasure to give instead of receive when we came to our Christmas Party."

And so on and on, over and over again, came letters in the same vein as these. Teachers continued to reiterate the values derived by their pupils from taking part in such service activities. Briefly stated, these values are growths in some of the knowledges, skills, and attitudes which fit children for effective living as citizens of one world.

78

Service Activities

SOAP, CANDLES, AND AFGHANS. Pioneer skills are revived as twentieth-century children make soap, candles, and afghans. Once again, these ancient skills meet a real human need. This time the need is not on the American frontier, but in far-off Korea. There, a few more people will know cleanliness, light, and warmth because of the efforts of American children. Since these projects are only now being launched as this chapter is being written, no complete reports are as yet available save the word that U. S. school children are "animated" as they gather the "makings" for soap and candles, and "zealous" as they laboriously learn the art of knitting.

3. *Children earn and save money for giving*

Projects which involve the giving of money have, like the Hallowe'en, Mitten Tree, *Check-po*, and other projects, been planned with a two-fold purpose in mind: to help meet overseas need and at the same time to enable American children to grow in a feeling of responsibility for others, even though those others are half a world away in strange lands. In evaluating the educational significance of money projects, we again turn to reports from teachers.

CHRISTMAS THE YEAR AROUND. Said one teacher: "This check that I enclose is our gift to CHRISTMAS THE YEAR AROUND. We earned our money by selling homemade candy. Below is what we would like to have you buy and send where needed: 2 pairs of scissors, 2 dolls, 2 balls, a song book, 2 packages of crayons, 3 checker sets, and 2 boxes of blocks." Do you see the picture of that group of Pennsylvania children as they engaged in the activities of (a) choosing the project, (b) making the candy, (c) selling the candy, (d) counting the money the whole class had earned, and (e) planning the expenditure

79

of this money for overseas gifts in terms of what they themselves would like to receive?

VALENTINE DIMES. It was an Arizona teacher who reported on another kind of earning activity, in which each child found his own "employment" and then contributed to the Valentine Dime Fund. Ways and means of earning money were varied, including extra chores at home, washing windows for neighbors, and lawn work and gardening. An eleven-year-old boy who sold cookies to a grandmother was astounded when, after tasting the cookies, *she* asked *him* for the recipe! And thus happy rapport between younger and older members of the neighborhood became an important by-product of this overseas project.

Because this teacher was, herself, a wise and sensitive person, she did what all good teachers do when children participate in money-raising activities. She was extremely careful to safeguard the child who had only a little money to give, as well as the child who could make a large contribution. She also placed emphasis upon the *group's* total fund, rather than upon individual gifts.

HELP KOREA! Following the Korean war three Korean money projects were organized: "Let's Buy a Book for a Child in Korea," "Let's Buy a *Soopawn* for a Child in Korea," and "Teen-Agers Can Help Korean Children." Interest was keen. Once again children proved highly imaginative as they found ways to earn money. Selling vegetables, fruits, and flowers (which they themselves had raised) proved lucrative for boys and girls living in either town or country. City children dashed off on errands to the store and on occasion washed the neighbor's dog, in order to increase their money for sharing. In some quarters it was reported that the fee for dog-washing increased with respect to the size of the animal!

In the matter of *saving* in order to share, teachers sometimes used the following approach. Rather than urge their pupils to "give up something," they threw out this challenge: "Before you buy yourself a 'treat,' ask yourself, 'Which will I really enjoy more, eating another candy bar, OR helping to make a Korean child well and happy?'"

Leaders of children tried to reduce money gifts to small, manageable amounts that had reality for children. Then it was possible to say, "Fifteen cents will buy three cokes, OR it will provide enough medicine to keep a Korean child free from roundworm for one year; 25¢ will buy five candy bars, OR it will provide vitamins for a Korean child for one month."

An important by-product of this project was the help children received in learning to be accurate and honest as they earned and saved for "charitable purposes." With guidance, children were led to realize that it is important to:

(1) Keep careful accounts of all the money they spend and receive, asking at least two other children to check their figures to be sure there is no error.

(2) Pay back to parents the money or materials with which they started. One teacher put it this way: "Suppose you made fudge. After selling it, repay your mother for the sugar, chocolate, milk, and butter used in making the candy. Then the money you have left will be really yours to share."

(3) Continue to do, *without pay*, their usual home chores. "If your parents know that you want to earn money to help Korean children, they will probably be willing to pay you for *extra jobs*, those over and above the ones which you do as your

regular contribution to family life." The teacher who made this suggestion received appreciative words from parents!

The above paragraphs indicate some of the many facets of "sharing." Now, let us turn attention to another.

Gifts from Overseas. For more than a decade, children of others lands have sent to America a wide variety of gifts— gifts as beautiful and as thought-provoking as the Japanese painting and the German transparency described earlier in this chapter. From their meager resources, boys and girls growing up in war-torn countries have produced pictures and fashioned dolls and toys of remarkable grace and beauty.

Why did they thus exert effort and make sacrifices in order to send gifts to us who have so much material wealth? We believe it was because they wanted to express thanks for the food, clothing, shoes, books, toys, and games that American children had shared with them. We believe that the sending of gifts was also prompted by the universal desire to make presents for somebody else. Furthermore, the young artists of other lands probably wished to tell us about the customs and traditions of their own lands.

American agencies receiving children's gifts from overseas have endeavored to circulate them as widely as possible, realizing that our boys and girls ought to be aware of the gratitude felt by foreign children, to have the experience of being receivers as well as givers, to discover that children in other countries have much to share with Americans—their ideas, skills, folklore, and traditions—and to learn that sharing is a two-way process occurring between equals.

Source Materials. In addition to the visual aids described in the preceding paragraphs, the following materials are available at a nominal cost from the American Friends Service Committee. The listing of what is provided by this one agency is indicative of the type of resources available from other, similar organizations.

1. *A kit for parents and teachers: as children share*

In this one envelope a teacher will find these materials for curriculum enrichment: detailed information about a variety of service projects, including those mentioned earlier in this chapter; patterns and directions for simple, inexpensive gifts that school children can make to send overseas; stories and pictures, plus a few songs and games; worship resources of a non-sectarian character; an annotated bibliography, and a list of visual materials.

Although this kit was prepared for the use of elementary school teachers, those working with children under six and over 12 have often made satisfactory adaptations. In fact, even adults enjoy working on the projects in this kit. Grandparents, parents, and children have found deep satisfaction and happy fellowship together as they made soap, constructed checker games, and wove afghan squares.

2. *Special packets*

Teachers increasingly realize that many of our holidays are appropriate times for emphasizing world-mindedness. In view of this, two seasonal packets have been developed by the American Friends Service Committee: *It's Hallowe'en* and *Mitten Tree*. The stories, pictures, songs, and detailed activity suggestions in each packet help to enrich the project.

Because of the wide-spread concern for the plight of Korea's children, following the Korean war, a number of organizations prepared packets or kits filled with materials suitable for use

83

in the elementary grades. *Korean Packet* is the name of the collection issued by the American Friends Service Committee. This packet contained not only the project suggestions cited above, but also background material about life in present-day Korea.

3. Booklets

If You Were a Child in Korea is the name of a picture-story booklet filled with stories, games, photographs, life drawings, recipes, and accounts of Korean customs—all geared to the purpose of giving American children a glimpse of child life in post-war Korea.

Mitten Yarns interprets the Mitten Tree Project described previously in this chapter. Included in it are photographs of a few of the thousands of children in other lands who have received mittens sent by American boys and girls. Particularly charming are the letters and drawings from foreign countries.

God's Children Care and Share has been found an acceptable booklet by pupils of all faiths. The stories, biblical selections, prayers, and songs which were selected for inclusion emphasize the universal fatherhood of God and the brotherhood of man. In public school classrooms and assemblies, portions from this booklet have been found helpful in the deepening of moral and spiritual insights as service activities were carried forward.

Books Are Bridges is an annotated bibliography of books for children from the pre-school years through the sixth grade. The books listed are those which help the young reader grow in knowledge and appreciation of persons of varying cultural backgrounds. Publisher and price are listed for each book.

Conclusions. In retrospect, we envision an assortment of simple things: spools of thread collected on Hallowe'en, homemade mittens hung on a schoolroom Christmas tree, a kettle of hot soap about to be formed into bars, a handful of jingling coins, an exhibit case packed with paintings and dollars from half a dozen countries, a booklet of stories and pictures, and a page of directions for weaving. These are some of the ingredients which, taken together, comprise service activities of children.

To the casual observer they may appear a hodge-podge of trivia. But to a sensitive and imaginative educator, these everyday items take on an uncommon luster, shining with a special kind of glory. To such a teacher, they are means to an end of the utmost importance: helping children grow in understanding and friendship toward other members of God's world-wide family.

SERVICE ACTIVITIES IN THE SECONDARY SCHOOL*

Some of the aforementioned service activities conducted in elementary schools may be adapted for use in secondary schools as well. In actual practice, however, the emphasis is different, and problems arise which merit separate treatment.

Giving Money. Collections or drives for individual contributions to various organizations are among the simplest and most obvious kinds of service activity. Some of the organizations performing international services for which such drives are commonly conducted are the Red Cross, CARE, Save the Children Federation, and the American Friends Service Committee. The drives may be schoolwide, or they may be or-

---

* The editor is indebted to Mark F. Emerson, Head of the Social Studies Department, Friends Central School, Philadelphia, for the preparation of this section.

ganized within a class. Sometimes they are spontaneous and informal, and in other cases they are periodic and highly organized.

The multiplicity of opportunities for giving has led some schools to bring some of them together in one inclusive annual campaign after the pattern of the community chest. A budget may be set up by a pupils' service committee for the organizations for which the school will campaign. Quotas are assigned to classes on the basis of the number of pupils and the average contribution needed to meet the budget. Collectors are appointed in each class. A pupils' publicity committee prepares posters and assembly announcements.

This is an efficient method of handling collections and probably brings in more money than separate drives for individual organizations. It also offers the students who conduct it a good opportunity to gain organizing experience and helps the whole student body to acquire early the habit of giving. It has several disadvantages, however. The temptation to compete for the biggest collection is one. The giving should be for its own sake, of course, and not to bring honor to one's class or to prove its superiority. There is also the danger that high pressure methods may be used, causing some students to give just because it is being done and they do not want to be different. When this occurs, the giving experience is of little benefit to the giver. Furthermore, giving money can be too easy, as when the money is merely passed out by the parent or is part of a generous allowance, so that no sacrifice is required of the student. Campaigns for giving have their place in schools, but other kinds of opportunities for service should also be provided.

Service Activities

Raising Money. Money may be raised for international aid through such activities as giving plays and concerts or conducting sales, fairs, or carnivals. A novel method used by one school is the holding of an auction of used toys at Christmastime. Pupils bring their discarded but still usable toys to be auctioned at the school by student auctioneers to their classmates. The proceeds go to the selected cause. The dramatic and musical clubs of another school annually raise enough money by their productions for the tuition of visiting students from their school's affiliated school abroad. (See Chapter 7.) Many of these activities are spontaneous and informal outgrowths of classroom work. An eighth-grade geography class, while studying China, "adopted" a Chinese war orphan by raising money to support the child for three years.

Raising money in such ways gives pupils an opportunity to do more than just passively contribute. An incidental advantage of a fair or carnival is the active participation of everyone connected with the school. In one school each class, the faculty, the alumni, and the parents' association each conduct one booth at the annual fair, which is followed by a picnic supper served by the mothers. After the supper each class puts on an act in a variety show. The whole school works together and is united as at no other time in the year, and the students learn to lose themselves in activity that is helpful to others.

Collecting Clothing and Other Material. Collecting used clothing for distribution abroad constitutes an important service activity. In some cases a campaign is conducted at a given time each year. March and April are good months for a drive because then winter clothes that are outgrown can be contributed instead of being put away for the summer, and summer clothes that are found to be no longer needed when taken out of their winter storage place can also be brought in. In some schools clothing is accepted throughout the year, a chest being provided for deposit of garments at any time.

One school sends out cards to every student's family telling about the need for clothing, with participation thus becoming a family and sometimes a neighborhood affair. To give students a part in and an understanding of the actual distribution of clothing given to the American Friends Service Committee, individual classes in some schools spend a day at the Committee's warehouse, helping to sort and pack the clothing for shipment abroad. Other materials collected by schools include school supplies and sewing materials.

Making and Doing. Even more valuable to the student than the foregoing activities are projects in which he gives time and effort to make or do something for others. These involve sacrificing more than money or clothing, which in the latter case may no longer be of use to the donor anyway. In addition, undesirable attitudes of superiority and self-righteousness often arise in connection with a service in which the chief activity is the impersonal giving of money. Projects in which the students get to know those they are helping, as through affiliated schools (see Chapter 7, "Affiliations between Schools of Different Countries") and in work camps (see Chapter 8, "Work Camps"), are most effective in discouraging such attitudes. By far the most significant types of service activities by the students are these two types of projects, also.

There are other ways, too, in which students may give time and effort in making and doing for others, although most of these are related to the community rather than the world scene. One school gives parties for underprivileged children and for the aged. Another brings children from a settlement house for an annual Christmas party at the school. Crippled children are brought to one school to attend games and plays. Students of a country school chop wood for needy families in the community. Sewing kits, dolls, soap, scarfs, caps, and afghans are made by various schools for shipment abroad.

Organization. Elaborate organization of service activities is unnecessary; in fact, the spontaneity of informal projects is to be prized. In some schools service activities are centered in a service committee, with membership open to all. Each class may have official representatives, or the committee may be made up of representatives at large from the entire school. There are usually one or more faculty advisers. Sub-committees may be in charge of specific activities, such as a school affiliation, a clothing drive, or a fair. Such a committee may add strength and continuity to service activities and have a strong influence in the school. Its efforts may be less spontaneous than those arising from individual or group concerns, but the committee need not interfere with these, and indeed, can encourage them.

Outcomes. What are the results of all these activities? It is obvious that a great deal of good is accomplished. Hunger is relieved. Needs are filled. Suffering is decreased. Many who are in need of friendship receive it. Thus, some of the bitterness, friction, hatred, and strife in the world is removed, and the cause of good will and peace is strengthened.

But the benefits are by no means all to the recipients, as we have seen. The young people acquire a more sympathetic understanding of others, including those of other economic groups and other countries. Reality is brought into many subjects they are studying, and their horizons and attitudes are thus broadened. They acquire the habit of service, develop

89

social conscience, and discover the satisfaction of losing themselves in the service of others. All this helps make them better, happier citizens of their own community, their nation, and the world.

SUGGESTED READING

Ballou, Richard B. "Education and a Point Five for Mutual Assistance." *Harvard Educational Review,* 23:51-59, Winter 1953.

Carr, William G. *et al. International Education Through Cultural Exchange.* Proceedings of the International Education Assembly. New York: School Executive, 1945.

Kenworthy, Leonard S. "Developing World-Minded Children." *Childhood Education,* 27:77-81, October 1950.

United Nations Educational, Scientific, and Cultural Organization. *In the Classroom with Children under Thirteen Years of Age.* N. Y.: Columbia University Press, 1952. Pamphlet.

Ward, Douglas S. "Education for World Understanding: Suggestions from Educational Service Abroad." *Progressive Education,* 27:197-205, May 1950.

5

Current Affairs Teaching and the Development of World Understanding

ERNEST F. SEEGERS

Any worthwhile teaching of current affairs will add to the student's understanding of the world and its peoples. Moreover, any classroom job that is well done in this field will contribute to the student's growth as a mature person. The object of this chapter is to suggest certain emphases in secondary schools in the presentation of current affairs to young people which will serve to develop world understanding, and to suggest a few ways in which the presentation can be made.

Most schools today recognize the teaching of current affairs as a responsibility, and make more or less regular arrangements for it. In some schools the major responsibility for teaching current affairs is given to the teachers of social studies, who may devote one period or part of one period each week to a discussion of current affairs, using various techniques. Many

Figure 15. A history class discusses the current world scene. Courtesy of George School, George School, Pennsylvania.

schools have regular current affairs programs for assemblies of the entire school.

Some schools may feel that time cannot be spared from an already crowded program for any regular attention to current affairs. It should be realized, however, that a certain amount of learning about current affairs is going on in the minds of all young people, for they do not stand still in their thinking on vital concerns. They are constantly exposed to opinions and reports. Their parents, their teachers, their athletic coaches, their friends in everyday life, the radio, the television, the daily papers—all these are constantly giving youth an education of some sort in current matters. Hence, it is important for a school to consider what effect its program is having on its pupils' attitudes toward world affairs. This is especially pertinent today when schools are becoming increasingly interested in developing citizens whose sense of responsibility includes the welfare of peoples all over the world. Obviously, the opinions and ways of thinking about current affairs which are being developed in young people today will affect their thinking in years to come.

This discussion does not propose to treat all aspects of current affairs teaching. Fortunately, such treatments have been undertaken and should certainly be consulted in a thorough consideration of the techniques of current affairs teaching. *The Teaching of Contemporary Affairs* (Twenty-first Yearbook, National Council for the Social Studies, 1950) contains excellent articles on various aspects of teaching current affairs in elementary and secondary schools and in junior colleges. A valuable survey of current affairs teaching in the United States is entitled *Current Affairs and Modern Education: A Survey of the Nation's Schools* (*The New York Times*, 1950). Both of these works are musts for teachers concerned with improving their teaching of current affairs.

FIVE AIMS

In order to help develop young people who are world-minded, current affairs activities should be directed to achieve the following aims:

(1) To broaden the horizons of young people so that they will recognize more people as fellow humans, will appreciate them and sympathize with them as such, and will recognize the interdependence of all nations.

(2) To develop an awareness and appreciation of the many

creative and positive efforts that are at present being made to bring peoples together.

(3) To build the desire for participation in and support of constructive action.

(4) To open up new lines of thought—new approaches to world problems which may not have been considered heretofore.

(5) To encourage students to base their judgments and actions with respect to current affairs on a system of values which transcends national boundaries.

These five aims need not be the exclusive framework for current affairs work in any school, but neither should they be neglected. The following pages will develop them in detail and suggest a few specific examples of ways in which their realization may be attempted.

CURRENT AFFAIRS TEACHING CAN BROADEN HORIZONS

The study of current affairs can help American youth realize that the peoples of all countries are essentially human. Although it is a simple fact, this elementary truth tends to be obscured merely by reading certain headlines and cartoons, by listening to those news accounts which daily proclaim that "Russia" wants to do this, or "Germany" will do that; that "the West" favors this, and the "Reds" demand that. In the case of the Soviet Union, for example, the students at one school in 1953 were tremendously stimulated by a personal account given by a newspaper editor recently returned from a brief visit to the Soviet Union. His calm and rational account, given to a school assembly and then to smaller groups, emphasizing the human and sometimes amusing incidents of his trip, and expressing his conviction that the Russian *people* he met were genuinely friendly, served powerfully to re-assure the boys and girls that, despite the actions of the Russian government, the Russian people are, after all, human. To many students this was a new slant on Russia, for they had not previously thought of distinguishing the people from the government.

Broadening of horizons is perhaps best brought about by personal reporting of this sort. It can be done by foreign students, studying in the vicinity and invited to spend a day at school, or by young people from other countries in our own schools. If politics are put aside for a bit, and they should be at times, and if questions are encouraged about other aspects of life, a great deal of enlightenment can take place in a short while. One does not have to tackle the most controversial countries. Accounts of life in Britain, in Mexico, in any country at all, will have the same general effect.

Reports by respected members of our own student bodies who have had unusual opportunities can be effective, such as those by returned work-campers, exchange students, or members of international-living experiments. These can be of a formal nature in assemblies or classes, or of an informal sort, such as at the lunch table.

Occasionally, it is well to tackle the more controversial countries. In recent years reports from China given by re-turned missionaries or relief workers have had a different ring from the average press accounts. In the days when Tito's Yugoslavia was almost entirely suspect in the United States, personal reports from that country differed from press accounts, also, revealing strong sentiment for freedom of speech and religion and a desire to break from Russian domination.

The opening of new and fresh outlooks can also be accomplished by other techniques. Foreign broadcasts can be recorded on tape for replaying in class, government information agencies can supply films on their respective nations, and much can also be done by well-chosen readings. However, the authenticity of a personal account is a more powerful agent. The interest and attention of boys and girls are held by personal anecdotes, as they would not be held by abstractions and generalities.

Horizons are also broadened when current events are presented, not as isolated events, but in their own background and setting. A series of film-strips put out each year by the education department of *The New York Times* is of value in this respect. Taking each month an important current subject, this series provides a film-strip and an extensive teacher's text with bibliography on the subject and its background. The device can be well used in the classroom and can also be adapted for shorter assembly talks.

There are several groups of weekly newspapers for young people which also do a good job in these respects. *The Scholastic Magazine*, the *American Observer*, and *The Weekly News Review* feature many valuable articles. Their publishers are to be commended for their intent to be objective, listing both sides of issues, and in their success in presenting the background of the news.

CURRENT AFFAIRS TEACHING CAN DEVELOP AWARENESS OF EFFORTS TO BRING PEOPLES TOGETHER

In order to develop world understanding teachers should give publicity to creative and constructive work that is going on—work which, with some exceptions, receives little publicity from the usual news media. We refer to projects like the village development program in India, which is under the joint sponsorship of the Indian Government and the United States Government and is aided also by private groups, such as the Ford Foundation and the American Friends Service Committee. This project, and those under the technical assistance program of the United Nations and under the specialized agencies of the United Nations, are especially newsworthy.

Projects such as these, unspectacular and lacking in sensation as they are, are usually neglected by our popular news journals or are relegated to the back pages, and yet they are actually some of the most significant grass-roots peace work now being attempted. With government backing for non-military projects apparently going into partial eclipse in the United States, it is even more important to give publicity to undertakings participated in by private agencies and by the United Nations.

The extensive exchange of students and teachers under the United States Government's Fulbright program and under literally hundreds of other programs of lesser scale is certainly of great significance. Programs developed under the Ford Foundation for developing area experts, for broadening the backgrounds of thousands of high school teachers, and for improving living conditions in backward regions should be known. The American Friends Service Committee and other religious groups have interesting projects going on in countries all over the world. The CARE organization, the Near East Foundation, the Houses-for-Korea project, and many others have constructive stories to tell that can give young people a sense of hope and faith.

Since these current affairs do lack the elements of ready appeal that make for front page attention, they are best treated with a bit of drama when presented to a class or an assembly. One interesting class session was addressed by an executive of the CARE organization. Since he was able to draw dramatically from a wealth of personal experience, he not only was convincing about the worth of the program, but he made it clear that all people have three great desires—to eat well, to be clothed and housed well, and to give their children greater opportunities than they themselves have had.

A series of dramatic programs on the work of individuals in the service of the specialized agencies of the United Nations has been sound-recorded under the title of *The U. N. and World Affairs.* These are of interest especially to the upper elementary- and junior high-school grades and can be obtained from local World Affairs Councils.

An effective dramatic program based on actual United Nations discussions about various African questions, entitled *Shadows over Africa,* is available from the Foreign Policy Association. This program is acted out by a large number of the audience, reading from scripts, and will hold the attention of an advanced group. Various films and filmstrips are also available on the work of the United Nations.

CURRENT AFFAIRS TEACHING CAN BUILD INTEREST IN CONSTRUCTIVE ACTION

Teachers can encourage the desire to participate in and support that which is constructive and creative—and the teacher knows when he has succeeded in this respect when he hears the question, "But what, if anything, can we students do about this?"

Of course, this degree of interest will not always be forth-coming. For one thing, some subjects cannot be easily brought to the pupil's level of understanding. Moreover, many who feel a sense of responsibility will not mention it. Teachers should bear in mind, however, that all students in a few years will be taking part in public affairs, and the degree of interest and effectiveness with which they do enter in as adults may be largely determined by their school experiences.

To the question, "Can young people in high school be effective in determining public questions?" Spahr Hull, director of high school activities for the American Friends Service Committee, relates how three high school students visited a Congressman to discuss with him a proposed bill for universal military training. The Congressman stated immediately that he was in favor of the bill and would be glad to discuss it with the young people. They then asked his opinion about several questionable sections of the bill, referring to actual copies which they had with them, whereupon it appeared that the Congressman had not read the bill carefully. When he did so, he expressed dissatisfaction with the wording of these sections. After a 45-minute discussion, he announced that, while he was still in favor of a system of universal military training, he was not going to vote for that bill, and he did vote against it.

We can point out to young people that one never knows exactly what and how much any action will accomplish. Certainly not all groups will persuade Congressmen to change their minds, but when groups of students interview or correspond with responsible persons in public office, the students at least acquire a sense of respectful familiarity with their representatives and an experience of participating in a democratic society. As a result, they should have a new feeling of the ap-

99

proachability of their federal government and a heightened interest in it.

Class trips to Washington, engaged in as a tradition by many high schools, can be made much more worthwhile than mere sightseeing trips. Interviews with officials can be arranged easily and real discussions with them carried out. A unifying theme for the trip can be selected by the group, signifying a subject they want to find out about, and if the subject is one of international scope it can be of special significance. Opportunities for visiting the United Nations headquarters likewise can be made more vital if one or more interviews with persons in the organization are arranged.

Some feeling of discharging a responsibility and of participation can be had by writing letters, as individuals or groups feel concerned about matters of legislation or policy. The following letter was written during the Korean War by an eleventh-grade class committee and approved by the class to be sent to a congressman:

The Honorable _____
The House of Representatives
Office Building
Washington 25, D. C.

Dear Congressman _____:

    As students of the junior class at _____ School, we have felt a deep concern about several of the current issues and problems facing our United States Government.

    We should first like to beg you to further and encourage all plans for negotiations with both the Soviet Union and China. It seems to us that the prospect of peace is completely untenable if the United States does not put forth all possible efforts to settle these problems peacefully rather than by open warfare.

Our second concern is the prospect of draft for 18-year-olds. We have discussed this question fully, and have not been able to reach a conclusion. We would appreciate it very much if you would send us your own views and ideas on this subject. We have also raised the question: if 18-year-olds are old enough and mature enough to be drafted, to go to Korea, to fight and perhaps die, are they then not old enough to vote and to help choose their own government?

Finally, we should like to see at least one billion for every ten billion dollars be spent for foreign aid. Is this so very much to ask for construction, considering all the United States Government is now spending for destruction?

Peace is something which all of us must give our lives working for, and we of the younger generation do not want to grow up in a world where it is known only as an impossible ideal which was given up about the middle of the century.

Directly in line with developing world understanding are all the many valuable activities related to school affiliation programs, such as packing of parcels, engaging in class exchange projects, work camps, and community chest drives. These activities are discussed thoroughly elsewhere in this volume. There is little, if anything, on today's educational scene of more value. Current affairs teaching can stimulate interest in such participation.

CURRENT AFFAIRS TEACHING CAN OPEN
UP NEW LINES OF THOUGHT

Teachers can contribute to world understanding by opening up new lines of thought and new approaches to human affairs which may not have been considered heretofore by young people.

In this respect we must recognize that our usual news media do not feel sufficient responsibility to emphasize the critical, the creative, the thoughtful in their presentation and interpretation of the news. Even our better papers give second section or back page coverage to much of this kind of interpretation and commentary. The average news media present stereotyped, matter-of-fact reporting of events—good as far as it goes, but specializing in the tragic and the despairing and neglecting current thinking and creative planning. They rarely present more than a summary of press association releases, and this alone does not help the cause of world peace. It encourages an outlook which accepts what happens as inevitable; it discourages critical thinking, confidence in mankind, and the desire to participate in the constructive events of the day.

In order to counteract the stereotyped nature of news reporting as our students are apt to get it if left to their own devices, our schools must be alert to independent news media and other sources which will carry the different, the contemplative, and the critical.

Among the daily newspapers in the United States, the *Christian Science Monitor* is perhaps outstanding in this respect. It has a staff of able and independent writers who frequently contribute positive and thoughtful feature articles, often about foreign nations and the United Nations. The editorial policies of this paper and its policy of avoiding the merely sensational tend to make it useful. It also gives attention to little known but constructive projects which are going on in various parts of the world.

Other leading dailies, such as *The New York Times*, the *New York Herald-Tribune*, the *Washington Post*, and the *St. Louis Post-Dispatch* also give attention to the critical and the interpretative. These papers are of course valuable ones, not only with respect to general news coverage, but also for their feature articles, which give insight into situations. Their Sunday magazine supplements are especially good in this respect.

A refreshing perspective on the news is afforded American readers by the editorial pages of a good foreign newspaper, such as the *Manchester Guardian*. Available in an airmail edition at low cost, this paper should be at hand in social studies classrooms or in the school library.

The suggestions of Mr. Justice William O. Douglas about a more positive voice for the United States in world affairs might be cited as the type of critical thought that is needed to supplement our reading of strictly factual reports. His views have appeared regularly in the independent magazine, *The Progressive*—a journal which should certainly appear with the more usual periodicals in classrooms and libraries.

The Nation and the *New Republic* have long been helpful as prompters and suggesters in the field of independent news comment. The Jewish *Commentator*, the Catholic *Commonweal*, and the Protestant *Christian Century* are outspoken in applying religious principles to the interpretation of current events. Two Quaker journals, the weekly *Friends Intelligencer* and the bi-weekly, *The Friend*, also frequently run suggestive articles in this field.

There are various journals in the category of limited circulation papers whose main purpose is to interpret current affairs according to their relevance to world peace. One of the finest jobs of reporting and of giving objective background on issues before the national government is done by the *Washington Newsletter* of the Friends Committee on National Legislation. A little bi-weekly paper edited by Charles A. Wells, entitled *Between the Lines*, attempts to comment on world issues from a Christian frame of reference. The British publication, *Peace News*, comments on developments affecting world peace as viewed from abroad. These smaller papers are the "salt of the earth" in the field of news journalism. Our students should know of their existence and should become accustomed to examining them for helpful opinions.

Since we cannot count upon all news sources to develop a world point of view, teachers must be alert to locate and introduce to young people such journals as those mentioned in the preceding paragraphs. They may succeed in opening up to their students new ways of thinking which they would be unlikely otherwise to experience. Teachers then will be encouraging their students to be alert, critical, and trained in the mature handling of sources of information.

CURRENT AFFAIRS TEACHING CAN DEVELOP JUDGMENTS BASED ON UNIVERSAL VALUES

In teaching current affairs we should encourage students to base judgments and actions on criteria derived from a basic system of universal values, rather than on any system of nationalistic values.

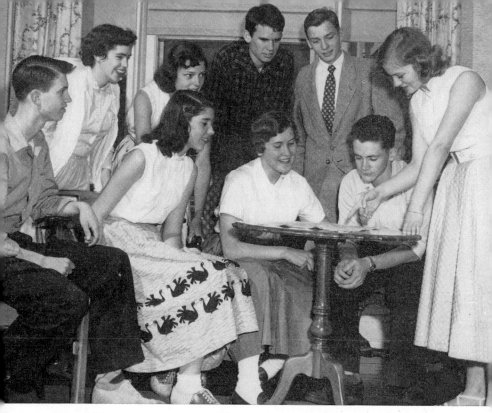

Figure 16. German exchange student uses map to explain current happenings in her country. Courtesy of George School, George School, Pennsylvania.

In this connection it might be helpful to point out that most guides to teaching published in the United States these days, and most lists of desirable educational objectives drawn up by school systems, teachers, or departments include a reference to developing loyalty to the values and institutions of democracy as one of the prime objectives of all education. This is certainly a worthy and basic objective, and our schools are doing what they can to realize it. Responsible teachers have the warmest feeling for this aim, truly carried out.

It is possible, however, that there are distinct limitations, even dangers, inherent in the type of thinking which, in the name of democracy, turns our education more and more to strictly nationalistic ends. It is not enough to teach democratic spiritual values if, mayhap, the following overtones are also developed: that great values exist only in society as found in the continental United States; that democratic spiritual values should be uppermost in our domestic society, but should not be applied to our foreign relations, which relations should be conducted only in a context of expediency and power; that the peoples of undemocratic nations are less human and hence inferior to the people of the United States; that the democratic doctrine which holds the individual sacred must of necessity at times not apply to individuals beyond our boundaries; that peace will only be possible when the other nations are much more like the United States.

A broader basis is necessary to prevent a narrow nationalism. What is needed is emphasis on a system of values which is without national connotations, such as one based on Christian ethics, or, simply, on the Golden Rule. If the individual is to be held sacred, then he is sacred all over the world, and his slaughter or degradation can only be deplored, not justified. He may be a citizen of an undemocratic country, but he has as much right to existence and enjoyment of life as we have. There may be critical need of food in a great country, and our Congress may delay meeting the need out of our plenty on the grounds that the stricken country is not "on the democratic side." According to a loyalty to democracy as a national fetish, this action might be justified, but it is out of keeping with a universal system of human values. Today the need is for the universal, according to which our current actions and policies should be judged. We will help develop world understanding when and if we develop in young people a loyalty to universal values of brotherhood.

This discussion does not suggest a specific formula for the teaching of current affairs, nor can there be one. Like all teaching, current affairs teaching is an art, practiced more or less successfully by teachers according to their peculiar talents, incentives, and background. The results of teaching elude exact evaluation. Possibly this is especially true of the question under discussion in this chapter. For example, how can one evaluate the effects of a current affairs program presented to a large audience of students? Some may not understand it, some may be too immature to appreciate it, some will soon forget it, but to this person or that it may help to open a new horizon, or give a measure of reassurance about his fellow men, or lead him to creative thinking.

Perhaps the social studies teachers should be considered the key persons in a school program aiming to develop world understanding through the teaching of current affairs. It is certainly true that well-grounded, alert teachers, skilled in leading discussion, are essential. Nevertheless, an administration which is keenly interested can be of great help by backing projects with personal encouragement and administrative prestige; by seizing opportunities to invite unusual assembly speakers, commencement speakers, and parents' day speakers; by helping to work out schedules of trips and special events, and by encouraging projects of teacher and student exchange and school affiliation. In addition, the responsibility for developing world understanding cannot be delegated to any one department or group of teachers. While the social studies teachers are especially involved, specific classroom work in current affairs can also be developed in English, foreign language, and art classes. Furthermore, the student's informal contacts with teachers of all subjects, with administrators, and with office secretaries and other school personnel are often of even greater influence than classroom work. In short, there is not a department or a person in a school who does not have the opportunity to help develop the world outreach of young people.

REFERENCES AND MATERIALS FOR TEACHING CURRENT AFFAIRS

Professional Journals
Social Education. National Council for the Social Studies, 1201 Sixteenth Street, N. W., Washington 6, D. C.

Social Studies. McKinley Publishing Company, 809-811 North 19th Street, Philadelphia 30, Pa.

Periodicals for Use by High School Students
American Observer and *Weekly News Review.* Two weekly papers. The *Observer* is for upper high school grades, the *Review* for lower. Civic Education Service, Inc., 1733 K Street, N. W., Washington 6, D. C.

Senior Scholastic. A weekly newspaper. Senior Scholastic, 351 Fourth Avenue, New York 10, N. Y.

Supplementary Journals and Magazines
Atlantic Monthly. Atlantic Monthly Co., 8 Arlington Street, Boston 6, Massachusetts.

Between the Lines. Charles A. Wells, publisher and editor, Box 269, Demarest, New Jersey.

Christian Century. Christian Century Foundation, 407 South Dearborn Street, Chicago 5, Illinois.

Christian Science Monitor. Christian Science Publishing Society, One Norway Street, Boston 15, Massachusetts.

Development of World Understanding

Commentary. American Jewish Committee, 34 West 33rd Street, New York 1, N. Y.

Commonweal. Commonweal Publishing Company, 386 Fourth Avenue, New York 16, N. Y.

Foreign Policy Bulletin. An Analysis of Current Affairs. Foreign Policy Association, Inc., 345 East 46th Street, New York 17, N. Y.

Friend. Contributors to The Friend, Inc., 304 Arch Street, Philadelphia 6, Pennsylvania.

Friends Intelligencer. Friends Intelligencer Corporation, 1515 Cherry Street, Philadelphia 2, Pennsylvania.

Harper's Magazine. Harper and Brothers, 49 East 33rd Street, New York 16, N. Y.

Manchester Guardian. Manchester Guardian, 55 East 51st Street, New York 22, N. Y.

Nation. Nation, 333 Sixth Avenue, New York 14, N. Y.

New Republic. New Republic Inc., 301 N. Street, N. E., Washington 6, D. C.

New Yorker. New Yorker Magazine, 25 West 43rd Street, New York 36, N. Y.

Peace News. Peace News, 130 Brattle Street, Cambridge 38, Mass.

Saturday Review. Saturday Review Associates, Inc., 25 West 45th Street, New York 36, N. Y.

Washington Newsletter. Friends Committee on National Legislation, 104 C Street, N. E., Washington 2, D. C.

World. World, 319 East 44th Street, New York 17, N. Y.

Films and Recordings
American Friends Service Committee, 20 South 12th Street, Philadelphia 7, Pennsylvania.

Anti-Defamation League of B'nai B'rith, 212 Fifth Avenue, New York 10, N. Y.

Development of World Understanding

New York Times Film-strips on Current Events. A series of eight each year, on large issues, and with accompanying text and bibliography. Office of Education Activities, New York Times, 229 West 43rd Street, New York 26, N. Y.

United Nations Films. A Catalogue of United Nations Films. Department of Public Information, United Nations, New York.

Information services of foreign nations, such as:
British Information Services, 30 Rockefeller Plaza, New York, N. Y.

Government of India Information Services, 2107 Massachusetts Avenue, N. W., Washington, D. C.

SUGGESTED READING

Clark, Delbert, editor. *Current Affairs and Modern Education: A Survey of the Nation's Schools.* New York: New York Times, 1950.

Cummings, Howard H., and Harry Bard. *How to Use a Daily Newspaper.* Washington, D. C.: National Council for the Social Studies, 1949.

Kinney, Lucien and Katherine Dresden, editors. *Better Learning Through Current Materials.* Stanford: Stanford University Press, 1949.

Payne, John C., editor. *The Teaching of Contemporary Affairs.* Twenty-first Yearbook of the National Council for the Social Studies. Washington, D. C.: National Council for the Social Studies, 1950.

Wesley, Edgar B. *Teaching Social Studies in High Schools.* Boston: Heath, 1950. Chapter 20, "Utilizing Contemporary Affairs."

6

School Assemblies

ROBERT E. EATON and LUCINDA ILIFF

In some schools assemblies are the periods to which pupils look forward for entertainment, amusement, or recreation. The assembly is an escape from the routine of learning into a relaxed situation where thinking may stop and where inattention or noisy misconduct may pass unchecked. The situation is quite otherwise, however, in schools where teachers see the assembly program as an extension of learning into the framework of a larger group. The assembly provides an opportunity for children to develop some procedures which cannot be learned easily in a classroom and to practice, on a large scale, certain skills learned in the smaller classroom group. Assemblies can be used to carry forward the whole school program and to interpret its underlying philosophy, and should be valuable personal and group experiences for the children.

It is clear that a great deal of thought about and planning of the assembly program are necessary. Too many assembly schedules consist of a hit-or-miss series of presentations from individuals and agencies wanting a chance to be heard. The schedule should be based on a survey of the central purposes

Figure 17. A student talks on current United Nations activities. Courtesy of Germantown Friends School, Philadelphia.

of the school and on consideration of methods by which pupils of a range of grades derive the greatest benefit from being together as a group. As teachers go over their own curriculum plans and see opportunities for programs, they can work out plans with their class or homeroom groups. To provide balance and organization, there should be a committee who can integrate the entire year's program. This committee may consist of pupils with a faculty sponsor to whom suggestions may come from any pupil or class. The committee gains valuable experience in evaluating aims and in devising ways to carry them out. They become aware that the responsibility should be divided among many and requires a ready spirit of cooperation.

OUTSIDE RESOURCES

A good starting point for the assembly planning committee in planning programs dealing with world understanding is to compile a list of persons in the community who have had contact with other cultures. There may be alien residents, naturalized citizens, refugees, exchange students, or exchange teachers willing to talk to the pupils and perhaps show pictures, costumes, or other articles from their homeland. A particularly fruitful assembly program was conducted in one school which had on its staff an exchange teacher from a school in Hawaii. The pupils thus felt direct contact with a school in another part of the world, and as a result continued the contact by writing to pupils in the Hawaiian school. Upon the return of the original teacher the next year, the school was able to follow up the assembly of the year before by hearing of her experiences in Hawaii.

Another valuable experience occurred when a former teacher returned, shortly after the war, from a year in Poland. She had brought back a great deal of material, such as native dolls, costumes, and other objects. A follow-up came when the school packed Christmas boxes with toys and useful articles for the children of Poland.

Many Americans who have traveled abroad are pleased if they are invited to show their pictures and to talk in assembly. Often there are pupils within the school who have been in other lands or among other cultures and have had experiences worth sharing. It is important, however, to discuss with speakers in advance the topic of the lecture and the ways in which it will be used by classes that hear it. Whenever possible, teachers should tell their pupils about the guest and the program in advance. Another important aspect of this kind of assembly experience is the classroom discussion afterward to clear up any misunderstandings and reinforce the basic idea of the brotherhood of man.

Besides individuals, there are organizations which are glad to cooperate in providing speakers and films. The Junior Red Cross, the United World Federalists, American Friends Service Committee, National Council of Christians and Jews, fellowship houses, churches, synagogues, community chests, and international service clubs are all glad to suggest or send speakers. A caution: In general, there are few adults who can speak effectively to children in the lower age groups without some prior suggestions from teachers. It is often helpful to remind a speaker to simplify his vocabulary, avoid introducing too many ideas, and avoid condescending to his youthful audience.

There are available numerous lists of films and film strips (see pages 34 and 59) which depict life in other lands and which may help children to understand other countries. Without care on the teacher's part, however, such films may give children unfortunate ideas about foreigners, such as that foreigners have queer, antiquated, or stupid ways of doing things. In one film on farming in India, for example, it would be very easy for false impressions to be formed unless, following the showing, each teacher points out the reasons why cattle are not eaten and why the farmer has a difficult time making a living. It is important, therefore, for teachers to preview the pictures, discuss them beforehand with the pupils, and point out certain features to look for. Afterward, there should be time for questions and discussion, either in the assembly room or in class. It is probably wise, also, for the pictures to relate to timely events. For example, during Brotherhood Week,

Figure 18. Through dramatization American children learn customs of other cultures. Courtesy of Philadelphia Public Schools.

Henry's Backyard is excellent material. The film gives a clear picture of mankind's likenesses and is an excellent springboard for discussion in grades one through eight.

RESOURCES WITHIN THE ELEMENTARY SCHOOL

It is probable that most schools will draw more extensively on the talent within the school than on that of outsiders for assembly programs. Indeed, so much benefit can be derived from a class-made project that no school need feel handicapped by lack of money for films or speakers. Grappling with problems involved in preparing assembly programs is one of the best ways for boys and girls to learn how to work together. It is also an excellent way to make classroom work helpful to a much larger group. A recent school assembly program consisted of creating an operetta through the united efforts of grades one through six. A pupil-faculty planning committee was the coordinating group. The theme evolved was man's progress through invention. Each class took an aspect of it and developed it to fit into the total picture. The coordinating committee sat in on class discussions, arranged timing, and had music written by the pupils. The show developed into an interesting one-hour production depicting man's struggle for a better life. The children learned how some three hundred individuals may work together to make a unified whole, and how, during the preparation, each one gives his ideas about the dramatization. For example, each participant can learn to listen carefully and be willing to give up "my" idea, if it is not in harmony with the central theme. The process of learning to understand other points of view and to evaluate one's own is an important step toward international goodwill. Thus the means —friendly cooperation—by which the program is prepared can help toward the end—tolerance and understanding of others. So the final presentation in assembly may be viewed not only as motivation, but also as the last step in the learning process.

RESOURCES WITHIN THE SECONDARY SCHOOL

In secondary schools, teachers often fear that preparing student assemblies consumes a great deal of time that might better be devoted to the subject matter of the course. With careful thought, however, a topic for an assembly program can usually be found that is worth extensive study and will enrich the subject matter. Assembly presentations may also provide opportunities for the development of individual and group relationships which will prove more profitable than "sticking to the lesson" in the book. For example, a presentation of the signing of the *Magna Carta* can be dramatically portrayed. A study of the issues discussed at the United Nations can be graphically shown through an assembly program.

Some suggestions for time-saving in the handling of an assembly program are: (1) Reduce to a minimum the costumes and properties that are used and create an audience willingness to accept makeshift externals and seek the central idea of the program. (2) Use content that has been studied in class and can be quickly transferred to the stage.

In most schools the culture of other countries is studied. This affords wide possibilities for the assembly program through the dramatization of folktales, games, manner of dress, ways of making a living, preparation of food, education of children, or manner of worship. This understanding of various cultures is by no means confined to the English or social studies departments. Chemistry and science classes have opportunities to show the international scope of scientific discovery and progress. A class in mathematics could show the advantage to the West of Arabic numerals and the international value of the work of Descartes, Napier, and Einstein. Music classes can sing songs from other lands. Physical education classes may present folk dances, with accounts of the people who dance them. Art classes may show the contributions of other nations in our own community's architecture through the use of photographs or drawings projected on a screen in the assembly. A cardinal point to remember is to avoid letting the audience leave the auditorium with the thought that other nations are "funny." For example, a program dealing with desert people should make clear *why* they wear loose, flowing

Figure 19. Dramatization of a foreign folk tale. Courtesy of Oak Lane Country Day School, Philadelphia.

robes and why our own dress would not be comfortable under similar conditions.

Some schools have a variety of student clubs which could be encouraged to share their enthusiasms with everyone in the school. Many teachers have found that the club takes special interest in the preparation of a program if an expert from outside, perhaps a parent, can be secured to help in the early stages of planning. Skits about the stories behind the postage stamps in their collections, dramatizations of letters from pen-pals, and scenes to describe the scientific contributions of other lands to the development of automobiles, machines, electricity, and photography make exciting material. In one school, a fellowship club reported the success of an assembly program in which a Jew, a Negro, and a Catholic student told their predominantly white Protestant student audience of some of the school incidents of discrimination of which they were conscious. The effect of the program was both arresting and enlightening. The planning and putting on of this program by the fellowship club brought a real problem of living to the attention of the student body and resulted in its desire to do something about it.

A dramatization of a book such as W. L. White's *Lost Boundaries* can lead to understanding of race problems and the need for understanding peoples. Although it is concerned with the American scene, it can build goodwill on an international scale if there is appropriate follow-up and discussion. The general restlessness among the non-whites in many parts of the world reminds us that the whites are the world's minority people and there are many unresolved problems. National and international themes are inseparable in the area of race relations.

Panel discussions of controversial issues make effective programs. Such discussions explore a topic, clarify the issues, and perhaps arrive at a tentative answer to the problem. Subjects which have been successfully used for panel discussion are methods of strengthening the United Nations, United World Federalism, and ways to promote peace. Speeches should be short enough to allow time for the audience to question and challenge the panel. Another fruitful program is a weekly report by a student or teacher of an item from current history that shows people working together in contrast to fighting and killing one another which is so emphasized in newspaper headlines. Accenting positive items, as, for example, the international cooperation at the time of floods, earthquakes, and other

Figure 20. A panel discussion in an assembly on current affairs. Courtesy of Germantown Friends School, Philadelphia.

natural disasters, will train young people to think of news in a constructive manner.

PROGRAMS WHICH MARK RELIGIOUS AND OTHER OBSERVANCES

Interesting assembly programs can be centered around the observance of religious holidays in other lands or by various groups in our own country. For example, one elementary school developed a Christmas program to show the cultural groups that have contributed to the celebration of Christmas in its city. Each grade from first through sixth took a different national group. The children brought the results of their study, visitations, and work in music into a Christmas program that had deep feeling. For example, the second grade studied the

French settlers in the area, visited a French Catholic school, and joined the French school in singing carols. Then they reproduced some of these activities in their Christmas program with feeling and understanding.

The sixth grade centered its study on the Dutch Reformed Church and its influence. Preparation for the assembly included a talk by a minister of the church on the history of the Dutch reform movement, followed by a number of salient questions on the part of the children, study of the music of the church, and a real endeavor to fit what they had learned into the pattern of the larger assembly of the whole group. The resulting program was simple—but its roots were deep—consisting of the singing of a hymn of the church and a simple portrayal of "Sinterklaas Day."

Other promising celebrations for similar exploration are New Year's, the Passover, Easter, and the arrival of Spring. There are also an increasing number of "weeks" set aside to mark an idea, such as the United Nations, human rights, and human brotherhood, which are worthy of dramatization in assembly programs. The possibilities are well illustrated in an article by Mildred S. Boyington (see bibliography at conclusion of this chapter) describing a program of genuine educational value which marked Brotherhood Week in a high school of Portland, Oregon.

PROGRAMS WHICH MARK PATRIOTIC OBSERVANCES

In the observance of national holidays, a program can show that many countries, like our own, have heroes and hopes. The liberators, San Martin and Bolivar, had dreams of independence and equality as did Washington. Gandhi, like Lincoln, worked for justice for all classes. Memorial Day can be a symbol of all mankind's grief for the tragedy caused by war; and Veterans Day can be a symbol of all mankind's longing for peace. American children can develop a live devotion to their country and its ideals, while respecting similar feelings possessed by citizens of other countries for their respective homelands.

There are hundreds of heroes and heroines of peaceful service whose lives can be a source of inspiration to young people. In Mary Hazeltine's book, *Anniversaries and Holidays: A Calendar of Days and How to Observe Them*, 1928, there is a day-to-day calendar giving birth and death dates which are valuable for use in remembrance of the work done by men and women through the ages. This reference book lists independence and constitution days for other lands and important men and women in science, arts, mission work, and other fields. A number of bibliographies are included. The Speaks Series of biographical booklets by Leonard Kenworthy contains material readily available for young folks on such people as Jane Addams, Toyohiko Kagawa, John Byrd Orr, and Albert Schweitzer. Dramatizations of these international figures help children find heroes and heroines from whose lives they may gain inspiration. Broad tolerance and devotion to the ideals of brotherhood become real and vivid as they see how individuals have responded gladly and courageously to the needs of mankind.

PROGRAMS ABOUT THE UNITED NATIONS

One high school class that had been studying the United Nations and the Korean situation prepared a panel discussion to show the origin of the trouble, the points of view of the

Russians, Koreans, Chinese, Americans, and Europeans. They tried to show how the United Nations had been handicapped by national interests and suggested points at which more tolerant attitudes might have reduced the friction.

From a different angle, a series of reports in assembly on activities of the commissions and specialized agencies of the United Nations can show that a great deal of constructive work goes on quietly and constantly, despite the fact that the press emphasizes areas of friction and disagreement. Dramatization of the United States Point Four Program and the United Nations program of economic aid to underdeveloped countries can put these activities onto the personal level of what they mean to a simple farmer. Assembly programs involving the United Nations work of child feeding, its drive against illiteracy, and its work to stop epidemics can help children see the world's needs and how we can respond to them.

Understanding of the work of the United Nations for world peace and its efforts to create better living conditions for mankind should not be confined to high school students. Appropriate material can be found and adapted for elementary school pupils. The reader is particularly referred to Ethel Dodson's description of her sixth grade's assembly program, cited in the bibliography at the end of this chapter. Following three weeks of study and preparation, this class in a public school of Virginia produced a program noteworthy for its wealth of content, diversity, and interest.

Another school planned an assembly program with children as young as second graders in the audience. They dramatized a possible situation in which a representative of a disease-ridden country asked for aid from the General Assembly, and obtained it. The audience thus was able to develop a feeling of one aspect of the work of the United Nations. The class producing the program had the valuable experience of working out staging, writing dialogue in keeping with the United Nations framework, and cooperatively producing a program.

CONCLUSION

Learning world brotherhood begins in the slow and tedious steps of learning how to live and work in harmony with those around us. This, no doubt, seems self-evident to the reader, but it is so basic that it cannot be over-emphasized. Coming to appreciate the rights of those who sit beside them in assembly, boys and girls can improve their techniques in finding solutions in larger areas of friction. If a child can learn to disregard racial, religious, and temperamental differences and work happily with any other child in the class, he is started on the road to understanding people in other lands. Conversely, the child has little chance of approaching a real understanding of the problems of other lands and cultures if he fails to appreciate those of his classmates with whom he is in constant contact.

In every assembly designed to foster world understanding, teachers should be constantly watchful that the information acquired by the children brings understanding and sympathy. Learning facts about other cultures does not of necessity advance respect for, nor interest in them. Since school and classes differ, no ready-made assembly program is equally suited to all. Teachers should search diligently to find what particular learning experiences will contribute to understanding of others and to concern about peace and brotherhood.

SUGGESTED READING

Boyington, Mildred S. "An American Brotherhood Assembly." *School Activities*, 19:187,191, February 1948.

Dodson, Ethel. "The Story of the World." *Virginia Journal of Education*, 45:15, 26, March 1952.

Hazeltine, Mary. *Anniversaries and Holidays: A Calendar of Days and How to Observe Them.* Chicago: American Library Association, 1928.

Kenworthy, Leonard. The Speaks Series. Brooklyn College, Brooklyn, N. Y.: The Author, Pamphlets.

McKown, Harry C. *Assembly and Auditorium Activities.* New York: Macmillan, 1930.

National Education Association, Department of Elementary School Principals. "The Assembly Program as a Learning Experience." *National Elementary Principal*, 31: entire issue, December 1951.

Thompson, Nellie Z. *Vitalizing Assemblies.* New York: Dutton, 1952.

Voigt, Una Lee. "How to Organize and Present Worthwhile Assembly Programs." *School Activities*, 23:22-23, September 1951.

7

Affiliations Between Schools of Different Countries

A school affiliation consists of an active partnership between a local school and a school located in another land. The schools have an informal agreement to keep in touch with each other and they aim to create personal friendships between pupils and teachers. The partnership is free of legal and financial ties, yet the two schools feel the same friendly responsibility for each other that is felt by any person toward his neighbor. To encourage and facilitate such affiliations, the School Affiliation Service has comparatively recently been established by the American Friends Service Committee as one of its experimental approaches to education.

The Affiliation Service embraces the purpose of the American Friends Service Committee: to discover and demonstrate effective ways of peace in a world that has become dangerously expert in the ways of war. The School Affiliation Service builds on the thesis that experience is the best teacher and

126

Figure 21. Students from France, Holland, and Germany, guests of their respective American affiliated schools, meet for discussion. Courtesy of American Friends Service Committee, Philadelphia.

this Service therefore aims to offer growing boys and girls and their teachers the closest approximation to living internationally that the distance from the United States to other countries will permit. The partnerships between schools involve exchanges of things made and needed, of letters, of ideas, and of people.

The special aim of the School Affiliation Service is personal—that the individual personality may come out clearly in each contact. It is worked deeply into the faith and experience of the Society of Friends that, latent or active, the saving grace of divine love is a part of the being of all persons. Like responds to like when a free, sincere contact is made.

Hence, effectively affiliated schools in the United States and abroad, by working together, become an integrated framework for growth—growth from international curiosity to international understanding, from international understanding to capacity for international cooperation. Such growth is obviously basic to forming world-minded citizens—people who can live and work in peace amidst the local and national variations of world society. Twentieth-century statesmen, especially those in the United Nations, need such citizens' insight into the structure of international cooperation, as well as their intellectual and moral support.

ORGANIZATIONAL BEGINNINGS

Observant and thinking people all over the world could see clearly in 1945 and 1946 that the institutions of society were inadequate to prevent further world wars. Law, politics, military establishments, even education and religion were not geared to the great job of creating a just and durable worldwide peace. The United Nations and its related organizations, especially UNESCO, and the World Council of Churches were outgrowths of this recognition of urgent need. A mid-century peace effort became a reality.

A spirit of responsibility led many persons and voluntary independent organizations to experiment in the ways of peace. There were pen-pals and CARE packages. Junior Red Cross, the New York Herald Tribune Forum, and the Save the Children Federation were active in the schools. Committees of educators wrote books of practical suggestions for teachers, such as *Education for International Understanding in Amer-*

128

ican Schools (National Education Association, 1948). Numerous educational conferences discussed the situation; church and community enterprises sought courses of action.

Among these, the Overseas Schools Committee was founded in Boston in 1946 to select and help schools become permanent centers for promoting continuous international friendships through affiliation, mainly in pairs, in the United States and Western Europe. It asked the cooperation of the American Friends Service Committee in selecting suitable schools in France, Holland, and Italy by visiting them, and in including gift packages from the American schools in its shipments to Europe.

The first affiliation in Germany was established in 1947. In the United States, 191 schools had established affiliation with foreign schools by 1948. In that year the founder of the Overseas Schools Committee and its active executive officer, Dr. Alfred E. Stearns, Headmaster Emeritus of Phillips Academy at Andover, felt that his age and health demanded his retirement. During the completion of his work, he expressed the view that, despite the value of the generous gifts of food, clothing, and school supplies which American schools had been sending abroad, the fundamental purpose of preparing for peace would not be accomplished without the cultivation of international friendships through personal letters and other exchanges. The Overseas Committee asked the American Friends Service Committee to assume full responsibility and disbanded June 30, 1948, sending its files to the headquarters of the American Friends Service Committee in Philadelphia.

Guided by a sub-committee of educators, the American Friends Service Committee set up an office called the School Affiliation Service to help member schools develop their part in this far-reaching plan and to explain it to others interested in joining. To emphasize the personal quality of the relationship, visitors qualified by teaching or international experience or both were appointed to reach each European school twice a year. As schools in the United States were scattered all over the nation, one visit a year to these schools was envisioned. These visits were to be reported fully both to the partner school and the Philadelphia office. Its files, begun in Boston, became a growing record of the strengths and weaknesses of each affiliation.

During the year 1949, close to 90 per cent of the affiliated schools in the United States were reached by members of the American Friends Service Committee staff. Classes were visited, assemblies addressed, committees and councils consulted, and key people interviewed, to encourage great numbers of teachers and pupils to do something active for the cause of international friendship. Reports of visits were duly made, giving the Philadelphia office a more complete picture than had been possible before. The great variety that appeared in the tabulated results seemed to point to the fact that a goal had been set, but no pattern drawn. The later sections of this chapter record the more significant undertakings.

SELF-EVALUATION

The opening months of 1950 were devoted, in part, to an evaluation of the program. The evaluation was based upon the observations of the visitors in 1949, the judgments of a majority of the schools, the thinking of educational leaders with large experience abroad, and the reasons for the withdrawal of about one-quarter of the schools on the list of the Overseas Committee.

Schools of Different Countries

The evaluation revealed the following facts about the affiliation program. It is a potent medium for bringing international experience to students and teachers in elementary and secondary schools, both at home and abroad. It leads to many varieties of direct and significant international contact. It influences favorably the attitudes of individuals toward persons of other cultures. Schools that surmount the obvious difficulties are rewarded by intellectual and spiritual growth.

These findings represent a basic justification for continuing the program. They demonstrate that the American Friends Service Committee is justified in going beyond the usual general public appeal which is for international friendship and mutual understanding through charity or through classroom instruction in world history and world-mindedness. An affiliation does more. It makes a specific appeal by opening up personal experience as an educative force that can be applied in elementary and secondary schools.

Evaluation of an educational experiment is a continuous concern. Further steps are constantly discussed in both staff and committee meetings. The major values in affiliation have been reported by one of the evaluators as:

(1) At their best, even without face-to-face contacts, they can enable teachers and students in one country to encounter directly some of the feelings, habits, and thoughts of their own age-mates and professional colleagues in another country.

(2) An affiliation provides a framework for fostering such face-to-face international contacts under conditions which tend to make the experience contribute its maximum to understanding.

(3) Affiliation seems to provide an extremely good core to

which numerous other activities contributing to a broadened human understanding can be related.

The remainder of this chapter describes what affiliated schools are doing, or in some cases, what they are failing to do—all of which are essential data in a later, more objective evaluation.

DIFFICULTIES TO BE FACED

The experience of the School Affiliation Service and the brief history of the United Nations both illustrate the difficulties which confront able, well-informed, and sincere persons as they try to work out ways in which nations can cooperate effectively. In the affiliation program, each partner had to attempt to surmount such physical difficulties as distance, difference in language, the fixed requirements of curriculum, and crowded daily schedules. In war-torn Europe, schools are often located in partly destroyed buildings, or in temporary quarters, and have lost the equipment needed for both office and classrooms.

Such conditions are reflected in the reasons that have led nearly half of the original list to withdraw. New schools join from time to time as they come to understand the current outlook of affiliated schools. Some American schools had never conceived any responsibility beyond material aid. Others had been discouraged by delays in the mails and in shipping goods. Partners had in some cases, despite care in selection, been mismatched, making cultural exchange difficult. Faculty leadership sometimes failed to develop on one side or the other of the Atlantic. A few, both here and over there, believed that such a far-reaching development did not belong in the schools. Yet other schools, beset with similar problems, were able to cope with such difficulties, often with the aid of the School Affiliation Service and its staff visitors.

These schools, along with numerous other organizations, have regarded themselves as explorers of a frontier, the civilizing of which is as important to the security and welfare of the world as was the winning of the West, a century ago, to the United States. To them, the partners in affiliation are making a joint effort to explore this frontier and find a place to settle for a larger life, not by staking out a claim to acres of virgin soil, but in the minds and hearts of men, which is where wars begin and where true and effective defenses against world wars must be built.

The main barriers are psychological and intellectual. There is a national pride, a high appreciation of national sovereignty, and a fear that to live internationally may be destructive of a well-established order. There are sharp contrasts in the economic conditions of countries represented in the partnerships of schools, and marked differences regarding political, industrial, and military proposals for preventing war and building up peace.

Differing educational concepts also are found among the nations, sometimes embodied in law, and sometimes in opinions held by educators. Some hold that education is properly limited to preparation of the intellect. Others see it more broadly and believe that true learning makes itself felt throughout personality and that schools, therefore, are responsible for guiding the pupil in his social, vocational, and recreational interests. The cultural standards of Western Europe for highly educated people require the mastery of one or more foreign languages and, in general, longer hours, harder work, and more exacting examinations than are required by American stand-

133

ards. The European teen-ager is sometimes more mature intellectually than his American counterpart, has less time for sports, and is more restricted in social experience. University education and the experiences of early adulthood will alter these relationships, more along individual than geographical lines. A by-product of the affiliation can well be the development by Americans of fuller maturity in intellectual capacity and the development by Europeans of the special insights and skills needed by free peoples seeking peace and security through the cooperation of national governments in a United Nations organization.

What is the influence of the aforementioned obstacles upon affiliated schools, each in a partnership to explore this frontier of the mind and spirit? These obstacles are to be recognized as barriers which only time can remove and which, for the present, have to be surmounted. The exploring party consists of teachers and pupils whose concern for the future has developed because of current international tensions and the revolutionary mood of hungry peoples throughout the world. The partnership with a school abroad where a similar interest and concern exists provides an opportunity for constructive action. The best tool in an American school is an effective permanent organization, including both teachers and pupils, firmly backed by the head of the school. Without an organization, the affiliation remains one of the many projects in the activities program, dependent on the skill and interest of a busy faculty sponsor. It assumes the status of a personal rather than a school enterprise. An organized committee, however, can grow, as time passes, into a permanent agency for group planning, for pooling available resources, and for recording and applying the findings of experience. Its goal of international interest, friendship, and mutual understanding becomes a characteristic of the entire school, apparent in curriculum, clubs, and social life. In public relations it becomes a challenge to the spiritual forces of the community. It appeals to the fearless, the persistent, the tactful, who love life and whose vision of the future is based on faith and hope.

To surmount the several obstacles, the affiliations plan a lively traffic, both ways, in personal letters, photographs, books, works of art, community studies, recordings, and visits. These exchanges offer personal correspondence to individuals. To class groups they offer the chance to share studies in geography, history, and literature. Of particular value are illustrated studies of their home communities and of striking features of national life and culture. To the school as a whole come the partner's art exhibits, publications, and recordings of plays and musical events. To the community comes the opportunity to entertain foreign university students and other visitors to the United States. Educational authorities and the federal government have often given necessary help when asked about providing for pupils or teachers from the partner school to spend a year as guests of the home school, or as exchanges. These are unusual things in the communities of the United States and do not occur unless concern and organization combine. Even under our State Department's Foreign Exchange Program, the number of teachers and students exchanged is small.

The School Affiliation Service of the American Friends Service Committee is set up to assist a school's affiliation organization with information, suggestions, and opportunity for inter-school conferences. The United States headquarters of the Service in Philadelphia provides contact with the School

Affiliation Service abroad—consisting in 1955 of two full-time offices, Paris and Darmstadt. Other representatives in Rome and in Tokyo keep an eye on the four affiliated schools in Italy and the three in Japan. Pioneer work in England is being done by a member of Oxford University. These leaders are concerned persons, experienced either in education or Friends' service or both. They represent American schools and the deeply felt desire in our schools for a peaceful and just solution of international tensions. Their work is to visit the partner schools in their respective regions, meeting with teachers and pupils active in the affiliation and observing the quality of the relationship with the partner. If there is misunderstanding or disappointment, they try to set things straight or suggest remedies to the American partner, through the Philadelphia office. When the affiliated school is happy in its partnership, enthusiastic letters are received by the partner and the Philadelphia office. The European staff visitors also play an essential part in matching schools for new affiliations, and arrange conferences for teachers during the summer holidays. During the years 1946-49, when schools in the United States were concentrating on material aid, the staff visitors abroad proved to be a much appreciated cultural link with America.

Staff visitors in the United States have, preferably, served earlier as visitors in Europe and thus are able to interpret the partner in personal terms. In conferences of teachers and pupils in the United States, the staff visitors' broader experience and intimate knowledge of many foreign schools have a far-reaching influence on the thinking and on the conclusions reached.

On each side of the ocean, the visitors are the eyes and hands of affiliation in dealing with obstacles that can be removed such as misunderstandings, or breakdowns resulting from prolonged illness, or transfer of concerned teacher leaders.

A TYPICAL DAY'S WORK FOR A STAFF VISITOR

After two years in north Germany and Berlin, the staff visitor went to a public high school in the suburbs of Philadelphia, the partner of a girls' secondary school in Berlin. In an open letter to pupils and teachers in Berlin, she stated that their partner is located in a residential district comparable to Zehlendorf or Dahlem and that most of the residents own their own homes and go daily to Philadelphia to work in businesses or professions.

Welcomed by the handsome, black-haired teacher-sponsor of the affiliation, the visitor was turned over to pupil Joan, Chairman of the Affiliation Committee, who was to be her guide for the day. They went first to the principal's office, then to see a display of Easter objects from Berlin, arranged on a table in the front hall. There were little knitted covers for Easter eggs in the shape of chickens, like tiny tea cozies, a bulletin board covered with charming pen-and-ink drawings, and a photograph of Christa, the Berlin student who was to be a guest of the suburban school the following year. In a large study hall paintings from the Berlin school were on exhibit.

While visiting classes in English, world history, German, and problems of democracy, the visitor showed slides of German schools, cities, and scenery. In the home economics cottage, the visitor arranged a small exhibit of work from other German schools on the dining-room table and sideboard. These included a tapestry, a miniature set of Bavarian peasant furniture, photographs, and books. A geography class, which had recently sent to Berlin albums with pictures from each of the forty-eight states, came in to see these objects. The staff visitor later attended the monthly meeting of the School Affiliation Committee, 15 pupils and four teachers; the latter said little, leaving the discussing and planning to the students. The foremost subject was how to raise funds to pay for board and room of the guest pupil. The Committee adopted a plan for students to make cakes and offer them for sale in the business district of two nearby towns on a Saturday.

PERSONAL LETTERS

From its inception in 1946, an exchange of personal correspondence, teacher to teacher, pupil to pupil, has been a continuous part of affiliations of secondary schools. Exchanges of personal letters by elementary school pupils are not unknown, but class letters are usually better suited to children of this age.

The continuous relationship of the two affiliated schools makes a more helpful and stimulating environment for correspondence than that of the numerous pairs of pen-pals fostered by various organizations.

The experience of the School Affiliation Service has led to a widely-held opinion that correspondence among older pupils should be spontaneous and uncensored. It ought not to be presented as a desirable opportunity for everyone, but as something special for a deeply interested few. In order to impress this on the students of a certain Pennsylvania school, the affiliation committee prepared a list of suggestions for good correspondence. It said, in part:

One of the best parts of an affiliation, but one of the most difficult to keep up, is correspondence. We would like to have as many as possible take part in it, but you shouldn't start unless you:

—have an interest in knowing about people in other countries and a strong desire for a lasting friendship through personal correspondence.

—intend to keep it up.

—are willing to give an evening a month to writing.

—realize that if you quit it will be a big disappointment to your correspondent and a blow to better international understanding and friendship.

—can be patient if you don't get a reply every time, and will keep on writing even if you don't get an answer every time.

In another school, a special committee, composed entirely of students, surveyed the correspondents in their school one spring. They reported that about one-third of the student body were fairly regular participants, and then went on to outline obstacles to correspondence. These obstacles include the following, which seem to apply to any school: numerous activities crowd it out, too many students are poor letter writers under any circumstance, students have difficulty understanding the problems of living in a less luxurious economy than their own, and they often have hesitation about writing on religious and philosophic subjects. Art, music, and the theater were reported as subjects of successful correspondence.

A girl who reported her experience as a correspondent at a conference of several schools said that more can be expressed in writing than in conversation, either at leisure or while working.

An obstacle to correspondence which exists in European

schools is the cost of postage. International Mailing Coupons, on sale in United States post offices, can be exchanged in European post offices for stamps. See *Handbook of School Affiliation Service* for details.

Figure 22 (left). Class in a German school reads letter from pen pal in U.S. partner school. Figure 23 (right). French children prepare project for their partner school in America. Both pictures courtesy of American Friends Service Committee, Philadelphia.

Difference in language is a barrier to be surmounted in many affiliations. It applies least in personal letters by students in secondary schools, for in many European institutions English is taught so effectively that the boys and girls are able to read and write it and discuss books and plays written in it. Such correspondence makes the American the debtor. Japanese schoolmasters seeking affiliations declare their students, too, are able to correspond in English.

In affiliations of elementary schools, the problem of translation is usually solved by people in the community. Such a solution strengthens the tie of a school with its community.

Schools of Different Countries

In one school a ninth-grade Latvian refugee girl helped with German translations. In one west coast community a Japanese minister helped translate. A vice-principal in another school who had been a Mormon missionary in Germany translated letters from German correspondents. Another school has found a German guest student willing to take on this extra responsibility. A teacher in a school with an Italian affiliation decided the best thing to do was to learn to read and write Italian herself. Of course, language classes are a frequent source of translations, as are members of community and school organizations, such as parent-teacher associations.

The differences in economic status and social experience between partners have to be bridged as each new exchange of letters gets under way. Tact and insight often develop as friendship grows. Teachers who have lived or studied abroad can meet with the affiliation committee and explain much about the foreign region. Teachers who are themselves active correspondents are answering a deeply felt desire in the partner school for personal contact and soon qualify to guide their pupils in tact.

Frank discussion among the pupil correspondents in one of the partner schools enables them to share their experiences. This tends to raise the general level of the letters. A sub-committee on correspondence, meeting regularly, can bring the writers within a school together, discuss questions which have arisen, and seek guidance from teachers if no solution of an individual problem is forthcoming. Such a sub-committee can give publicity to the correspondence by supplying excerpts to the school paper, or for reading in assembly.

A rather dramatic example of the obstacles which will be overcome somehow if there is real interest in writing to a

141

friend in another land has occurred in a United States-France affiliation of two schools for the blind. Here the added problem of the need to use Braille as well as a foreign language entered the picture as an obstacle to exchange of ideas. Nevertheless, ideas were exchanged. The French school put them down in Braille; at the American end, the French Braille was translated into French, the French into English, and the English into English Braille. Here an especial eagerness for exchange is seen.

A staff visitor in an elementary school in Italy found that the children had prepared letters with little figures drawn on them, introducing themselves or telling of flowers and birds in the neighborhood.

Friendship developed through school affiliation often expresses itself in gifts, as does all good fellowship. It is only for the initial gifts that American children need advice. Answering a question about desirable gifts from a high school in Oregon, a staff visitor in Germany wrote: ". . . include snapshots, maps, scenic postcards, cancelled stamps, or stamps, or international clippings from local papers. All such additions are enthusiastically welcomed by German boys and girls. Snapshots of the letter-writer are preferable, we've found, to detailed accounts of height and weight, which have no meaning to the Germans and strike them as queer. It is best, too, for Americans to type their letters, or if writing, use ink. Pencilled handwriting is much harder for German children to read."

The School Affiliation Service makes no effort to measure the amount, the quality, or the influence of this voluntary correspondence. It is a person-to-person affair. In visits by the staff and in inter-school conferences, however, evidence bobs up of long-time effects of some of this correspondence. There is, for instance, a German university student who applied for a year's scholarship in the United States, giving as a reference the correspondent of his school-days. He attributes his winning in the competition to the letter which his American friend wrote.

A school girl of 17 in New England who had spoken with enthusiasm of her experience in exchanging letters with a girl of the same age in the partner school in the Netherlands, wrote up her story for the use of School Affiliation Service. Excerpts follow:

> We have been corresponding for almost *three years* now and *I feel as though I have known her all my life.* I write to her about every four or five weeks and she does the same. It usually works out that I receive a letter from her about every four weeks and then I immediately write back. The *first one or two letters* that I wrote to her and that I received from her were sort of *stilted and unnatural.* Now they are *friendly and casual.* The topics that I write to her about in my letters center *mostly* on *school activities;* my marks, the subjects I take, my extra-curricular activities, the annual Pageant, the annual Spring Fete, sports that I take during the year, and other things that have to do with this country in general. In the summer I have told her all about the camp I go to. This summer I will be a counsellor and so will have something new to tell her. I have sent her Christmas *presents* for the past two years and I have tried to send her things to do with the United States. I have sent her powder and a scarf with scenes of New York on it. I also send her the *magazines* that I subscribe to, *Seventeen* and *Senior Prom.* She has been quite thrilled with them and even her mother enjoys them.
>
> She in turn writes about her school activities, her extra-curricular activities and almost the same things I write to

143

her about. She has sent me many *pictures* and I have sent her many, too. Last September she invited me to visit her in Holland this coming summer. I would have liked to have gone, but that *trip* is to be postponed *until I am in college*. I have not said anything to her about visiting me here in the United States because I would not know how or when she would come or how her financial status would be.

The only suggestions I have as to continuing a correspondence is by writing every time a letter is received (at both ends). Make the letters interesting and friendly and casual. Europeans, especially those our own age, are very eager to write to "pen-pals" in the United States and to learn more about the strange country across the ocean. It is the Americans who say they will do something and then fall along the wayside.

I have had a very interesting time corresponding with her because I have found out that she is not much different from a normal American girl. But I have also received the impression that she (and most other European girls her age) are more interested in their education and family relations than the social aspects of life. They go to parties but they don't go to quite as many as American girls do.

Letters from teachers abroad and the observations of staff visitors indicate that this least organized and most individual part of the affiliation program is of real value, even if correspondence is maintained by only a fraction of pupils or teachers in a given school. It is an elementary step on the difficult road of international understanding and cooperation. To take a few steps opens the mind at least a little. Furthermore there is a subtle unmeasured spiritual influence within the affiliated school and its community growing out of every exchange that reaches the heights of a "warm friendship." Few individual pupils or teachers can contribute more to winning the frontier.

CULTURAL INTERCHANGES

Personal correspondence at its best deepens the foundation structure of a school's international program as we have seen. The friendships which it builds can be a pervasive spiritual force. Breadth, however, is accomplished by enlisting larger numbers of students in the preparation of interesting materials of educational value both to the producer and the recipient. Such cultural interchanges help to surmount the obstacle of distance. The variety of possibilities is so great as to require the coordinating and perpetuating influence of a well-established committee of teachers and pupils.

Some of the materials for these cultural interchanges are prepared for exhibit in the partner school; others are to be studied in the partner school's library, or in classrooms, studio, or shop. Paintings and drawings, samples of wood and iron work, records of popular music and newspapers are all particularly eloquent forms of expression among school boys and girls. Illustrated studies of local communities or regions, school systems, scientific hobbies, or national characteristics are highly educative both to the club or class that makes them and to the recipients. Once partner schools get a clear understanding of their mutual resources, they can make sound recordings for each other. Sound recordings open up an amazing variety of interchanges. In June, 1948, a German school boy addressed in English (via a recording) an assembly of his school's partner in Pennsylvania. The speaker voiced the thankfulness of his schoolmates for shipments of food and clothing (so much needed in those days), but emphasized that personal correspondence was more important. He hoped that the writers would not take a summer vacation from writing, but use their free time for more and better letters.

Figure 24. German boys enjoy a newspaper from partner school in Arizona. Courtesy of American Friends Service Committee, Philadelphia.

Among the particular duties of a school's affiliation committee are arrangements for exhibits and representatives at interschool conferences, held from time to time in regions where several affiliations are active. The affiliation office in Philadelphia asks each partner in the United States for frequent reports of what has been sent and received in the way of cultural interchanges. It is up to each school's committee to see that such reports are promptly made up and forwarded. There is a small cost to member schools for the preparation and forwarding of materials to partners, as well as for representation at regional conferences. Direct mail to the partner school abroad is generally used for forwarding projects. Particularly precious or fragile objects of art are sometimes forwarded to the Philadelphia office and cared for as personal baggage of an American Friends Service Committee staff member. This places on the school visitor abroad the responsibility for delivery, which is done either by mail or in person. It is a much slower way of transmission than direct mail from the United States.

Customs duties are sometimes embarrassing to the recipient, especially when unanticipated. There have been a few instances of the partner school in Europe having to meet such charges. The School Affiliation Service office in Philadelphia is the best available source of information on costs of shipping for large parcels or boxes.

Some projects planned well in advance may occupy the producing group for a considerable time. A ninth grade class in Pennsylvania wrote an illustrated book in five chapters entitled "Our Country Through Trips and Legends." Five pupils prepared the chapter on the Southeast, three worked on the Central portion, four on the Northwest, four on the Southwest, and six on the Northeast. The staff visitor who was to take the book to the partner school in Berlin wrote: "I read every word of it and learned a good many things about the United States and its legends which I did not know before."

A California high school affiliated with five secondary schools in a German town prepared and sent 3,300 Christmas greeting cards, each one signed by an individual pupil. Art students designed the cards, industrial arts students made the linoleum blocks, and the school's print shop produced them. An eleventh grade boy wrote the greeting in verse, chosen by school-wide competition:

147

Across the Atlantic this Christmastide,
Comes hope for peace that has not died,
Come many greetings that have not faded,
Come new ideas that are not dated,
Comes good cheer in a world of sorrow,
As we wait and hope for a better tomorrow.

An elementary school in Pennsylvania, affiliated with a school in France, made plans for the year of what to exchange, as follows:

Kindergarten—Used picture books, autumn leaves cut out of colored paper, Hallowe'en masks, and songs, the words and music of which were written by the children.

First Grade—Scrap book.

Third Grade—Scrap book of Hallowe'en and knitted squares for blankets.

Fifth Grade—Home-made stuffed animals.

Sixth Grade—School supplies, paper, pencils, erasers.

A private elementary school in California, also affiliated with a school in France, had the eighth grade girls dress four dolls representing typical elements in the population of California—white, Negro, Indian, and Mexican.

A school in New York State reported much interchange with a French school. From France came mounted specimens of autumn leaves and chrysanthemums; magazine pictures of bedrooms, automobiles, and singers of popular songs; a serial story; a large folio of fashions for women for each season of the year; cut-outs of girls' hair styles and clothes; a booklet of prevention of accidents; a large notebook on holidays in France; manuscripts of folk songs; sheet music of songs printed in the sixteenth century; an essay written in French; and class exercises on seeds, plants, algebra, English, and chemistry. Students of stenography sent numerous notes and post-cards written on a typewriter that the American partner had provided. For its part, the New York school sent mats, travel brochures, photographs, wall decorations, candy, pencil sharpeners, a Viewmaster stereoscope and reels, a microscope, and a written class project on life in the United States, illustrated by photographs and drawings.

The director of a German school wrote to the staff visitor that the partner, a high school in California, was preparing a picture book for beginners in the English language. He said, "It is being eagerly awaited by our youngsters who are very lively boys keen on learning English."

Another California high school received from its partner in Germany a carved wooden cuckoo clock. It was hung in the main office where crowds gathered to hear it strike.

A German school sent to its partner in Pennsylvania the first tape produced on their new tape recorder built by their physics instructor. It contained songs and greetings.

A school in Berlin sent to its partner, a boys' boarding school in New England, a history of the school, a map of Berlin showing the four sectors, and a summary of the current political history of the American sector of that city.

An elementary school in Italy sent to its partner, in Washington, D.C., a charming booklet containing samples of crocheted lace of various types of designs. The Washington fourth grade was fascinated by it, and seemed to think "it's the kind of things we Americans don't do." A later report cites a great variety of drawings, carvings, needlework, and household appliances. There is a doll dressed in Abruzzese costume, miniature copper pans, a terra cotta savings bank, ceramic pots, a collection of classified leaves of trees and

149

flowers of the region, and, finally, notebooks and compositions.

A staff visitor in Germany was taken by pupils of a German school to visit a toy factory. They began the tour as the saw first touched the wood, and followed along until the product was being packed in boxes marked "S.S. Kresge Co." and "Woolworth's." The factory manager picked out one of each kind of toy (which accumulated to a sizable amount) and gave them to the visitor, who then asked the manager to send them to the school's partner, a public elementary school in Pennsylvania.

An increasing use of sound recorders adds life and reality to the interchanges of educational material. A Pennsylvania high school, affiliated with a school in Germany, had a recording made of Christmas greetings, all in German, and one or two American Christmas carols. The record was packed in unbuttered, unsalted popcorn and sent by air express. It arrived in time to be played on December 20, before the school was dismissed for the Christmas holidays. As it happened, the Pennsylvania school played its copy of the recording over the public address system of the school on the same day.

A church school in Portland, Oregon, affiliated with a church school in Tokyo, Japan, received 400 Christmas cards, beautiful block prints made from wood cuts. The Portland School's acknowledgment was a recording of brief addresses by the presidents of the various clubs in the school and of each class. The minister of the Japanese Methodist Church in Portland was the first speaker on the record. The principal of the school in Tokyo replied that he had used his inter-room communication system so that all his students could hear it simultaneously.

A public high school in Philadelphia, affiliated with a school in France, prepared several musical selections for its partner school, including the Fred Waring arrangement of "The Song of America."

A public high school in California and its partner in Berlin have exchanged tape recordings of singing by their school choirs. After receiving a gift of clothing, the Berlin school wrote an illustrated thank-you letter with drawings showing the clothing in use. When California sent dried fruit in burlap bags, Berlin's acknowledgment was burlap transformed into tapestry by its ingenious art department.

The School Affiliation Service office records are enriched by reports on the reactions of the partner schools abroad. For instance, a large photo album prepared by students of the photography classes and other classes in a California public high school showed the typical school day in pictures of ten different pupils. These had been selected to represent the various courses offered in the high school and the differing national backgrounds found there. Three copies were produced for the three partners—a boys' school and a girls' school in Germany, and a Japanese school. One of these volumes was on exhibit at a workshop conference for teachers in Germany and became one of the most studied items on the table. Numerous questions were asked of the school visitors about American school life, and everyone commented on the feeling of reality which it conveyed. Their comments, reported by the staff visitors, are on file in the School Affiliation Service office.

A boys' boarding school in Virginia affiliated with a school in the Netherlands devoted an issue of the school quarterly to pictures and articles about its partner. It was planned long enough in advance so that copy could be prepared in the Netherlands and photographs gathered and forwarded. There were articles on "Our Town," "Our School," "Types of Dutch Schools," "A Study Evening," "Soccer in Holland," "Hockey," and "Liberation of our Town." The headmaster wrote, "The distance is too great for personal contact on a more extensive scale, but it is no distance at all for mutual sympathy. On a small scale we can thus be active in the spirit of the United Nations."

In a Philadelphia high school, affiliated with a school in France, the home economics classes prepared an album on child care. A staff visitor wrote, of the reception given it, "It made a tremendous impression and was gone through page by page with the greatest admiration and appreciation. The quality and ingenuity of the work was commented on, and the accomplishment by the American students will not only be used in all the English classes, but will also circulate in the technical classes as well. That is, in the sewing and cooking classes." Such a project has opened up to the French school an entirely new understanding of home life in the United States.

An interchange of school publications, including American high school yearbooks, is useful. These are usually produced to fit into the latest teen-age fads of dress and speech and often need interpretation to partners abroad as well as to grandparents at home. One of these high school yearbooks was studied and discussed in a classroom of the German partner. The boys were invited to write their reflections. One of them wrote in English as follows: "We peeped into the New World through a small slot when our American partner school sent us a 'yearbook.' The feeling crept over me, probably due to the expensive cover, that this book had been put out by people completely different from the people I was used to. Yes, the European is certainly different. Our school system as seen by

an American must look like a strait jacket. If we search for
a school in the yearbook, we cannot find the building. All the
pictures of school life are taken outdoors in what looks like
a park. This is symbolic of the unlimited liberty of movement.
From his youth, the American is educated to move independ-
ently and he is really called upon to use his ability. The young
American is not affected by the seriousness of life at too young
an age because his rich country does not force him to think
of earning a living as early as we must. It goes without saying
that we would be willing to change with the young people
across the ocean, but to set up their life over here, we have
neither the means nor the idealism. We ought not let ourselves be overcome with jealousy, however, for we cannot
change very much in our situation anyway. So we should
face the seriousness of our existence and accept the proverb,
'Working makes life sweet,' and try to like it."

How few school boys in the United States could reply in
German!

GIFTS OF MATERIAL VALUE

There can, of course, be no fair interchange, under present
conditions, by means of money. It is for this reason the interchanges, in practice, are in terms of educational value. Economic recovery is well under way in Western Europe, but
there still are situations, especially among refugees, in which
full employment is impossible, and many live on the verge
of destitution. Sound personal pride precludes asking for
money gifts, but a friendly relationship between partner
schools can make it possible, as is often done among close personal friends, to sense the need and plan together ways and
means of helping out. An independent boarding elementary

school sent CARE packages to its French partner. The directress of the French school wrote to the visitor: "Have I told you that a cherished dream has been realized? Parents of our pupils, class by class, have met at the school during January and February. It helps our children so much in their family relationships. At the first meeting 50 per cent of the mothers came, who often brought grandmothers and even aunts. We would never have succeeded in getting these parents together if we had not been able to offer as an attraction and in order to give the meeting the warm atmosphere of intimacy, the refreshments which we owed to the CARE packages. The children from each class themselves prepared the hot chocolate and cakes which they offered to their parents. How could one help listening attentively and openmindedly to the advice of the teachers and the directress when one is seated before the table covered with good things to eat? The parents talked freely with us and we sensed that we were able to help them. But what gave us the most pleasure at these meetings was the joy that the children had at seeing us receive their mothers, whom they often see disdained because of their poverty and their utter wretchedness. The children were happy and proud and I believe that it did them a great deal of good."

A public high school in California found out that the English library in their German partner school was not at all well equipped with the best samples of English literature suitable for their more advanced students in English. The result was the shipment of several copies of two new pocket-size editions of Shakespeare, *Four Great Tragedies* and *Four Great Comedies*.

A boys' boarding school raised $100 to send to the School

Affiliation Service office to buy UNESCO gift coupons for their partner in the Netherlands.

The teacher in a public high school in the state of Washington, in the first year of affiliation with a German school, sent over the supplies for a Christmas dinner for their colleagues abroad. The director of the German school wrote: "The ladies and gentlemen of the high school sent us for Christmas a splendid package in which there was everything that could be used for an effective party. It was held in our art room, which has in the meantime received new and radiant lighting facilities. It was really a marvelous party. Coffee and pastry were exquisite, but that which was given of the more spiritual nature you would have had to experience yourself. The entire affair was under the motto, 'We are going to see Seattle.' At each fairly large station along the way something special happened which was told and illustrated in an excellent and most humorous way. Our girls cannot be happier and noisier than this gathering of teachers was. But it is true: 'A teacher who cannot be happy in his heart, is a burden to himself and can be no real educator.' We also saw pictures from Seattle which Ingrid [an exchange student] had; they showed especially the life and activity among the students in the high school and found many responses."

Some schools in the United States found money gifts easier to manage than the cultural interchanges. A school in Germany received a gift of $65 from the teachers of its partner in Ohio. To give it a permanent value, the German school appealed to the Kultusministerium for aid and advice in producing a bronze plaque to be placed in the corridor of the school house. It was completed by a German artist. The school visitor found it located so as to exercise the maximum influence on the sensitive growing minds of the school boys as they pass by.

EXCHANGE OF TEACHERS AND STUDENTS

The United States has opened the way annually for thousands of visitors from abroad to see the country, get acquainted with its institutions—political, commercial, and professional— and study in its colleges and universities. The federal government and voluntary agencies participate in meeting costs and in arranging itineraries. In the realm of education alone, about 34,000 students came from abroad for the year 1953-54. (See the pamphlet, *Building Roads to Peace: Exchange of People Between the United States and Other Countries*, Office of Educational Exchange, Department of State, 1950.)

Work with experienced and growing affiliations emphasizes the fact that personal visits between partner schools by teachers and pupils make their school's association more real. Plans for vacation travelling by teachers and by parents have allowed for a stop-off in the town where the partner is located. Some schools invite guests from the partner for an entire school year. The first instance of this was when a Friends' boarding school in Pennsylvania had a guest teacher from one of its affiliates in Germany. Each year sees a few more schools taking similar steps. The School Affiliation Service makes information available in *A Guest Student in Your School*, in a companion pamphlet, *Sending a Student to Your Partner School*, and also in briefer form in sections J and K of the *Handbook of School Affiliation Service*.

Though an infinitesimal part of the vast influx of students and observers from abroad, these guests of schools gain a depth of experience in homes and community affairs which many others without such contacts miss. A school, moreover, provides a particularly appropriate starting place for an ambassador of goodwill. It is a nerve center of the body politic, representing a cross-section of the neighborhood. Its life always may be and often is characterized by a spirit which helps people rise to a high level of understanding and morality, an indefinable atmospheric life-giving force. The affiliation is a bridge between the visitor's intimate contact with the grass-roots of society in the United States and the homeland. But affiliation is more than a bridge. It is also a living thing growing out of minds and hearts to bring civilization to a spot on this new frontier of international relations.

The American Friends Service Committee does not look upon affiliation as an educational device to make young Americans acquainted with the outside world by brief contacts here, there, and everywhere. Affiliation is a long-term deepening experience which adds meaning to many other briefer associations with life abroad. This was illustrated in a large union high school in California which is a partner to four secondary schools in Freiburg, Germany. A visitor from another German city stopped at the California high school on a short tour with a prepared schedule of special purposes in mind. She set this aside to meet with the teachers and students comprising the school affiliation committee and interested them by her account of the school system and country of Germany. The local newspaper printed a picture of the visitor, the leaders, and affiliation staff visitors who happened to be at the school the same day. It has been arranged, on occasions, for teachers from a European partner, while in the United States on a three-months' tour of schools as guests of the Department of State, to include their affiliated school in their itinerary. One man from Berlin spent four days in a boys' boarding school in Connecticut, talking with the staff and boys individually and joining in class discussions. He wrote later: "Friendship and peace among nations must be started by and will always depend greatly on friendship between the individual members of those nations." The Philadelphia office is always ready to help bring about such occasions.

A DOUBLE VISIT:
FRANCE AND ISRAEL REPRESENTED

During a summer vacation, an elementary school in Pennsylvania played host to the directress of their partner school in France. She visited in homes, had a vacation trip with the principal and his family, and, when school opened, spent several days in the classroom. Her visit in the school overlapped that of a teacher from Israel who came to the United States under different auspices.

Madame, from France, was an expert in puppets. In the fourth grade, she found a wide-awake and eager group of beginners, to whom she returned again and again, teaching them how to manipulate a puppet to make it convincing to an audience and how to fashion costumes that were suggestive of character. The class, in return, presented her with materials needed by her puppeteers in France.

In the seventh-grade class in English composition, descriptions of summer experiences in camp, hobbies, and jobs were read. Madame asked for and was given the papers. She said, "This is what my children will want to know about your country. This shows how you really live. I'd like to read these to my English classes." The seventh grade also made recordings of their readings, of English poetry, to be accompanied by mimeographed copies of the poems.

In the school quarterly, after the visitors from France and Israel had both left, the principal wrote: "There is little doubt in my mind about the fact that many—perhaps all—of us on the faculty have been deeply enriched as people and consequently as teachers, by our contact with Yvonne. Again, as when we were with Immanuel Yafeh, we felt the world grow smaller; human beings everywhere seemed more alike than different; the dream of peace appeared as having roots deep within a final reality. It was reassuring, too, for us to have personal contact with teachers in other parts of the world working with the same educational philosophy, struggling with the same problems. . . . And if this could be true for France, Israel and the United States, might it not be true also for Iran and the Sudan and Pakistan and Uruguay and—even peoples behind the Iron Curtain? The thought is not new; the feeling giving substance to the thought gains a new intensity . . ."

A GERMAN-UNITED STATES TEACHER EXCHANGE

The first exchange of teachers between affiliated schools—Germany and a school in the state of Washington—has been followed with keen interest. The German teacher, after her return, wrote of her "wonderful experience that it is possible to become friends with people from such a different background, different experiences, different language, if both sides have enough good will to understand each other. And I have found so much of this good will and friendship in the United States that I cannot but think of your country but as a second home country."

159

The director of the German school wrote to the teacher from Washington four months after the close of her year's service in his school: "Though you are no longer among us, still the traces of your presence here cannot be eradicated. The American Room in which you taught has now become in the fullest sense a Reading Room; it is constantly gaining significance in a way which you can hardly imagine. We are constantly enlarging its usefulness, and are trying to give it more and more of a really homelike character, so that the pupils feel at home there. Our American Committee has undertaken this project." He wrote also of his own teacher who had spent the year in Washington. "The year was rich for her in experience. Though we here cannot change everything into the American way and pattern, still the pattern of America gives us inspiration to think over how far we can get new ideas out of these experiences. What has grown out of history, and what has proved practical through the centuries, one cannot toss overboard between today and tomorrow. But to enrich our traditions through the new influx of ideas, even from the outside, was ever a blessing."

In writing to the School Affiliation Service staff visitor, the German director mentioned one result of his colleague's frequent speeches. "The desire to understand America has been stimulated and many prejudices overcome that remained in the mind. The value of these exchanges is that our representative comes in contact with out-of-school circles and so the tie between both peoples becomes stronger."

Returning to Europe, the exchange teacher wrote an article for her school magazine, saying: "When people [in America] became better acquainted with me I came to hear that I in no way corresponded to the common conception held of the German teacher. They had thought of me as being older and somehow more impressive and corresponding more to their universal impression of what Germans are like. There was a deeply rooted notion, 'All Germans like to drink beer.' But, sorry, I don't like beer at all. Now these disillusionments were soon overcome and to make a long story short, we very quickly and completely understood one another. Each learned the more to prize and love the other, the more we discovered that no one stood up to the concept which the other side had made of him and his people. We realized that we are all human beings with very personal inclinations and qualities, weaknesses and excellences, and that it is often only necessary to become acquainted to understand one another."

She described advice given to her by the principal of the high school in their first interview, "Whatever comes up that you don't know about, let the kids do it." The German teacher was naturally somewhat skeptical about such advice, but: "My skepticism proved to be unfounded. Boys as well as girls were exceptionally helpful in explanation and in action. If anyone tried to make capital out of my European inexperience, it was always nipped in the bud by the class—thus, I learned an essential principle of American education which truly became gradually clear—namely, to lead youth to a feeling of responsibility in doing things by themselves—this practice is in accord with the facts that the pupils ask more questions than we are accustomed to in the German schools."

The various sources from which these quotations are taken refer also to the unattractive phases of American teen-agers as seen in school—the widespread practice of gum chewing in class and out, the dirty, rumpled garb of the boys, and teen-age speedsters in automobiles.

SECONDARY-SCHOOL PUPILS AS
EXCHANGES OR GUESTS

Many officials, both in government circles and among educators, have not favored including teen-agers in their plans
for exchanges. Boys and girls are assumed to be immature and
lacking in experience. The eagerness of youth, however, the
faith of teachers in their best pupils, and the typical American
readiness to experiment have led to approval and support for a
few programs involving a comparatively small number of
carefully selected, typical boys and girls. These programs all
recognize the necessity for complete planning in advance and
thoughtful preparation of the individual. The participating
agencies are finding that the teen-agers are, by and large, making good as ambassadors of goodwill. Unfortunate incidents,
due to the youth of the guests, are almost unknown. Temporary embarrassments are often prevented by the foresight of
the leaders and the advance preparation of the guests.

Among the voluntary agencies active in these programs are
the American Field Service and the Brethren Service Commission. The former began in 1947, screening applicants in Europe
and the Near East for scholarships offered by American
schools. The latter, in 1949, in cooperation with the Exchange
of Persons Program, Department of State, brought to the
United States 90 boys and girls from Germany and Austria,
placing them in homes of all denominations, as members of the
family attending high school for the year. The numbers have
been larger in later years. In 1952 several American boys and
girls were sent to German homes and schools. The Farm
Bureau, National Grange, National Catholic Welfare Conference, and the 4-H Club Foundation also have programs for

secondary-school students. The urban teen-agers Exchange Program for German high-school boys and girls only, with money appropriated by Congress and administered through the Department of State, has given substantial financial aid. Governmental funds for the exchange of American students or for American students as guests in schools abroad are not available except as raised by the participating organizations.

The fact that a European student who is preparing himself for university and professional life loses a year of school work if he becomes an exchange student or a guest (because of rigid European course requirements) is only an apparent obstacle. Many applicants feel that the experience is more important educationally than securing speedy professional preparation. Their testimony after their year in the United States bears this out.

In public high schools in the United States, careful arrangements are made as to the homes in which guest students will live. They are sometimes received as guests; other neighborhoods feel it better to raise funds to pay for room and board at prevailing prices, but in homes closely connected with the school. In one school district in Pennsylvania, the parent-teacher association held three community meetings inviting representatives from every organization in the township to attend—the Rotary Club, The American Legion, The Lions, The Scouts, and many churches. These meetings unanimously approved inviting a guest student and raising $700 through small individual contributions to pay for room and board. The money came in slowly but in time to guarantee arrangements for the following year.

Affiliation staff visitors abroad seek interviews with those students selected between the dates of appointment and departure. The *Christian Science Monitor* helps by giving complimentary subscriptions to them during the same interval. United States government officials in Germany have interviewed those selected to aid in their orientation.

Two person-to-person exchanges of students began in 1950-51, one of which accompanied the exchange of teachers, already noted, in the state of Washington. Such projects require the approval of the school authorities, and sometimes special scholarship grants. A Pennsylvania high school, for its first exchange boy abroad, raised funds for his traveling expenses. His family provided insurance and clothing; families abroad made him their guest.

To help member schools through the complex arrangements, and to make the experience of earlier exchanges available, the affiliation staffs in Paris and in Darmstadt each include a well-informed specialist. After a school has approved an exchange in principle, from nine to twelve months are needed to make plans with the partner, to raise funds, select and prepare the right candidate, and arrange transportation.

The director of a college in France, in a public address, recalled the benefits bestowed on boys in his school who, over a three-year period, had each spent a year in an affiliated school in Pennsylvania: "Three of our best pupils have returned transformed after their sojourn among you during a year which will be important in their lives. They are in an excellent position today to strengthen the bonds which join the youth of our two lands."

The director of a school in Germany wrote to the principal of a Friends' school in New Jersey: "We look with great gratitude to the friendly and pleasant receptions which our two students have found among you. Most of their letters express how quickly they have felt at home. We should like sometime to return this exchange and have some of your students come here."

A German boy, a guest at a Friends' school in Pennsylvania, found himself involved immediately in the whirl of American life. He longed for a day 48 hours in length. The boys and girls impressed him as comparable in social maturity to German university students. He noted that the relationship between boys and girls is quite natural. Nobody bothers to explain it. Both feel equal and expect the recognition due them. He found among his fellow students a definite pride in the achievements of their country, but they seemed to lack the binding feeling of belonging which he had in regard to Germany. He attributed that to the short period of American history and the great mixture of populations in the "melting pot." Here is his concluding sentence: "And what am I to my American friends? I am a German. Never have I heard a bad word in respect to what happened in former years."

The exchange girl from Germany to a high school in Seattle was interviewed by a staff member of the Philadelphia office on her homeward journey. She became devoted to the family who received her into their home, and spoke of them as "my American parents." Their daughter, two years younger, became her devoted companion. They had separate rooms but were always together in one room or the other. The family included her in all their social life and recreations. She felt that she had no difficulty at all in adjusting herself to her new life. Many things were new, but she felt equal to them all. As to the advice she might give to another girl having the same opportunity, her answer was, "Just be yourself." She was asked about her relationship with the Jewish pupils in the high school. Some of them, refugees from Germany, complained about the serious losses suffered by their families and themselves. As she and her family were refugees from Silesia, she could establish herself on the same basis; they were all alike in that they all had to start over again. After two months back in her German school she wrote to the staff visitor: "It seems rather strange to me to take so many subjects. School does not make me any difficulties though. In my last mathematical test I received 'sehr gut,' since I had learned all required problems in my last year's Math Analysis class. We often have hot discussions about interesting articles of the *Reader's Digest* or about government, society, or foreign policy of Great Britain. I am mostly starting these hot talks. Since we pupils in America had so much freedom to criticize or to express our appreciation in school or in private life, I can never hold back now. My knowledge of the American Constitution will sure help me a lot when we will learn newest German history. I lost all my self-consciousness about language and speak English almost as well as German, so will have no great difficulties in the university next year, where I am going to study English, French, and history. Besides, I am proud of my ability to drive a car, to play tennis, and to typewrite. During the two months that I am with my parents again, I got accustomed very well to German life. My biology teacher says that one would not know I had just returned from the U.S.A. when meeting me in school, since I look like everybody else, like a good little girl, only I seem to be much happier and livelier than one year ago. One thing was harder. I got much maturer, gained a lot of self-confidence. My old comrades had left the school, my new ones did not like me at first, as they tell me now. It seemed to them that I thought I was 'somebody.' By now I am feeling very happy again though."

166

One social note might be included, though connected with a summer tour rather than an exchange of students. A girl from a California high school affiliated with a school in Rome was able to locate the boy to whom a classmate of hers was writing. The result was a date or two which she enjoyed hugely. The leaders of the affiliation in the California school said that after her return she had given them a clearer picture of their partner school than they had received in any other way.

AFFILIATED ELEMENTARY SCHOOLS

From the beginning a few elementary schools have sought a place in the affiliation program. The number increases from year to year. A section in the *Handbook of School Affiliation Service* deals with elementary schools. Illustrations drawn from their experience have been used earlier in this chapter side by side with those from secondary schools. Exhibits from both levels have been shown in teachers' conferences. Conferences for teachers in charge of affiliation activities in American elementary education are held occasionally, sometimes for only a day and sometimes for a weekend.

An easy but superficial conclusion is that pupils in the lower grades are too immature in mind and unskilled in the arts of communication to profit by international contacts. The necessity of translating everything into the language of the partner school does, indeed, present a difficult problem. The rapid increase in elementary-school populations, resulting in added teaching and collateral duties, makes many teachers work beyond their strength.

The same spirit of surmounting obstacles, however, which drives secondary schools to explore the frontier of personal international relations, characterizes the concern of certain parents and teachers at the elementary level. They, too, regard as an imperative immediate duty for themselves and their children the building of a foundation in the heart and the mind upon which a peaceful world society can be established.

These teachers and their supervisors find that the whole world is within the horizons of even little children, for even these younger ones see parents traveling abroad on business and have friends and relatives in military or government service abroad. In their homes the children find illustrated magazines with pictures from all parts of the globe. In the effort of the school to give the younger boys and girls a gradually enlarging experience of their *own* land, there are numerous opportunities where our relationships abroad fit in naturally.

Hence, the experience which teachers have had with affiliation, even in the kindergarten, encourages other teachers, supervisors, and the American Friends Service Committee to explore the possibilities further. Pupils can acquire practice in reading and writing just as well when dealing with an international item as when dealing with a national or local one. Illustrated projects, such as scrapbooks aimed to acquaint the pupils with the life of their own land, are just the thing to send to the partner school. Group letters or photographs are welcomed by children of the same age level abroad. Some schools find that the boys and girls want individual correspondents. The letters are mailed in bulk as are greeting cards at Christmas and Easter, small friendly gifts, such as dolls, snapshots, or personal photographs. In one school in the United States the distribution of the contents of such a package from overseas is a gala day. Parents are invited and translators are ready. So carefully is it done that both child and family are notified in advance if a hoped-for letter or parcel did not arrive.

168

Figure 25. Five-year-olds examine dolls sent by French affiliated school. Courtesy of Oak Lane Country Day School, Philadelphia.

Music is a particularly appropriate field for exchanges. Recordings of school singing create interest. Words and music of songs popular in one school are often sent to the partner. Illustrated children's books with stories known around the world are of basic importance. *Little Red Riding Hood* in Japanese and *The Three Bears* in French were exhibited at one of the school affiliation conferences referred to in the first paragraph of this section. The opening of the mind by such experiences is as essential to education as the depositing of information in the mind.

The principal of a Philadelphia public school visited his school's partner in Germany and returned home with many group pictures. When these were passed around in the class-rooms, a third grader remarked, "Those children look just like we do." Earlier, the older pupils had written and produced a play. They had made it into an illustrated booklet for their partner school which reproduced it during the Philadelphia principal's visit.

The earlier conferences were delightfully surprised as one report after another revealed both breadth and depth in the international experience of the children. Continuity year after year gives depth; the breadth comes through the influence of the affiliation, serving as a magnet to draw together a variety of short-term visits and reports on readings and on family experiences. It gives childhood a consciousness of the setting in which the United States will have a large part to play for years to come.

CONCLUSION

The Second World War destroyed organized militarism in two great nations. The fear of war persists, however, and the institutions of national life have been making a great variety of adjustments to meet the threat. The result is fear and restraint. These fears and restraints, fundamental causes of war, cannot be transformed in existing world relations to open friendliness among people. On a deeper level than defense programs, forces that bind humanity together in mutual confidence and understanding must also be making adjustments to the times. Art and other forms of culture, scholarship and general education, religion and cooperation for human welfare—all free expressions of the human spirit—are expanding, but lack the support anywhere near comparable to that given to the armament programs of the world.

Schools of Different Countries

Concerned persons in education have created the affiliation ideas described in this chapter, coordinating those impulses which are native to art, learning, and religion, and helping focus those impulses upon international friendship. The affiliation idea was born in the mind of one of the very great educators of the previous generation, Alfred E. Stearns, Headmaster of Phillips Academy at Andover, Massachusetts for many years. Teachers and school officials, conscious of the present urgency of international relations and sensing the potentialities of school affiliations to affect the roots of human thought and action, have kept it alive. New schools have joined, under the leadership of equally concerned and far-seeing teachers. They have no established technique to guide them; they have not been specifically prepared for such a type of international education. Experience is teaching them that affiliation has the complexity of intimacy; it also has the flexible adaptation to circumstances that characterizes exploring parties in a wilderness.

When such teachers gather in conference as a small but intimate group, the affiliation movement finds itself. Its character tends to take form; basic thinking goes forward. Its spirit envisions a better world society. Holding such conferences is a foremost responsibility of the School Affiliation Service. The first international gathering took place in Germany in the summer of 1950. Such conferences have become a welcome climax for teachers in affiliated schools. The 1954 conference, held in the Netherlands, brought together teachers from seven countries. Delightful personal friendships resulted. Each conference becomes a memorable experience for French and German teachers who have in this way their first contacts since the end of the war. Says an American observer who has attended all the conferences: "We are making a real impact that is not only carrying school affiliation forward, but is furthering reconciliation and understanding between peoples. Through the impact on teachers, we reach out to the children who are in their hands."

Conferences within the United States have been too numerous to list. Though initiated by the School Affiliation Service, these conferences are more and more being planned by committees of teachers from the participating schools. Representative pupils and concerned parents often join these gatherings, which adds greatly to the inspiration and faith.

The sharing of opinion and experience by the teachers, and the exhibits which the sharing produces make clear that an affiliation adds meaning and content to much of the well-established work of the school. The classes in French and German, in geography, history, and other social studies are making the affiliation a novel and animating feature. Affiliation enriches the work of international clubs and UNESCO Councils. It has a very close relationship with service clubs and with public and religious organizations. The affiliation can moderate extremes of public opinion. Its actual experience with persons from other lands will make some people realize that antagonism to foreigners may not be wholly natural.

The American Friends Service Committee has no sectarian purpose in mind in sponsoring school affiliation. Nor has it any thought of seeking a permanent place for itself amongst the educational institutions of the United States. It is following a well established and widely publicized policy of readiness to investigate and support, through an experimental period, proposals which seem likely to contribute toward removing the causes of war and producing a more favorable climate for the peace that, in their hearts, most of the peoples of the world desire. If the experiment of affiliation is successful, it will find its way into established educational policy throughout the nation.

PUBLICATIONS OF SCHOOL AFFILIATION SERVICE, AMERICAN FRIENDS SERVICE COMMITTEE, PHILADELPHIA, PENNSYLVANIA

A Guest in Your School, 1953. Mimeographed pamphlet.

Activity Suggestions, 1950. Mimeographed leaflets. No. 2, Social Studies. No. 3, Foreign Languages. No. 4, English. No. 5, Sciences. No. 6, Arts. No. 9, Student Activities. No. 10, School Newspaper and Yearbook. No. 14, Elementary School. Other numbers out of date.

Alphabetical List of American Schools and their European Affiliates. 1954. Mimeographed pamphlet.

Handbook of School Affiliation Service, 1954. Mimeographed pamphlet.

School Affiliation, 1954. Pamphlet.

School Affiliation News. Four issues yearly. Mimeographed.

Sending a Student to Your Partner School, 1954. Mimeographed pamphlet.

SUGGESTED READING

Beale, Lathrop V. *Résumé of Report of a Study of the School Affiliation Program.* Philadelphia: American Friends Service Committee, 1953. Mimeographed pamphlet.

Kenworthy, Leonard S. "High School Seniors and World Mindedness." *Progressive Education,* 27: 205-207, May 1950.

——— *Studying France, Germany, Italy, and the Netherlands in Elementary Schools.* Philadelphia: American Friends Service Committee, 1953. Mimeographed pamphlet.

National Education Association. *Education for International Understanding in American Schools.* Washington, D. C.: National Education Association, 1948.

Niemeyer, John. Résumé of Report, *Looking Ahead in School Affiliation Service.* Philadelphia: American Friends Service Committee, 1953. Mimeographed pamphlet.

Schauffler, Marjorie Page. "School Affiliation—One Answer to a Wide Problem." *Educational Leadership,* 11: 424-427, April 1954.

Steck, Eliza Smith. *Report of International Teachers' Conference, Ommen, Holland, July 23—August 1, 1954.* Philadelphia: American Friends Service Committee, 1954. Mimeographed leaflet.

United States Department of State, Office of Educational Exchange. *Building Roads to Peace: Exchange of People Between the U.S. and Other Countries.* Washington, D.C.: Department of State, 1950.

8

Work Camps

DAVID S. RICHIE and GEORGE A. WALTON

Work camps are informal, temporary enterprises organized for the purpose of supplying young people of high-school and college age with the experience of group work for the benefit of others.

The first work camp was established by a Swiss pacifist, Pierre Ceresole, in 1920 near Verdun in France to provide adults of many nationalities with the opportunity to join together in clearing the rubble of the war and in building new homes for the peasants. This first international work camp, which was held as a demonstration of a more peaceful way of living together, has been followed by many further experiments with the work camp technique by various groups, in various parts of the world, for various purposes, and for a wide range of age groups.

The first work camp in the United States was held in the summer of 1934 and was sponsored by the American Friends Service Committee as an opportunity for college students to study the problems of unemployment, poverty, and racial tension in the Pennsylvania coal fields and to earn the right to do so by the sweat of their brows. They dug a reservoir and pipe

Figure 26. A bull session at work camp headquarters.
Courtesy of Social Order Committee, Friends Yearly Meeting,
Philadelphia.

line for a government homestead. Since that time, the Friends and others have sponsored camps for young people of high-school as well as college age; they have sponsored weekend and week-long projects, as well as summer projects; and they have sponsored work in areas of racial and economic tension, both in America and abroad. Agencies which have sponsored or operated work camps include churches, the federal government, universities, and public and private schools.

Those Americans who have had the opportunity to take part in work camps abroad have been relatively few, but they have had unforgettable experiences in joining with young people of other nationalities in a variety of projects. Work done has included removing debris caused by an avalanche in a remote Austrian village, repairing the damage done by floods in Holland, clearing land to be farmed by refugees near the Arctic Circle in Finland, landscaping grounds belonging to homes for delinquent Arab and Jewish boys in Israel, and building homes for refugees in Germany. Still other work has been done south of the border, in Mexico and El Salvador, where drainage ditches have been dug for the improvement of sanitation, trees planted to check soil erosion, and assistance given in vaccination and inoculation campaigns and similar projects.

Many Americans have found equally important opportunities in work camps nearer home—working in the summertime with Indians on their remote reservations, with minority groups in crowded sections of cities, and with migrant farm workers in rural areas. In addition, work campers have built health clinics, community centers, and playgrounds.

Still more young people have been challenged to participate in weekend work camps located in the worst housing areas of our largest cities. In Philadelphia, where this idea originated, more than 4000 young people have participated in one or more of the 450 weekend work camps held during the past 14 years, and the idea has spread far and wide—to Boston and Los Angeles, to London, Paris, Helsinki, and Tokyo.

NEEDS OF YOUNG PEOPLE SUPPLIED BY WORK CAMPS

Work camps are frequently the result of a demand for service opportunities on the part of young people eager to volunteer. They are the result of a more-or-less conscious need to be of service to others. There is usually little difficulty in recruiting; rather, there is a problem of too many volunteers without adequate leadership or suitable work projects.

What do young people growing up in today's world feel a need for? First of all, they recognize their need for *exposure*, for the chance to see what life is really like for many others less fortunate than they—what it is and ought not to be—full of poverty, exploitation, and struggle.

Second, young people are eager for *experience*, for opportunities to find out how good life can be—full to overflowing with comradeship, joy, and mutual aid.

Above all, young people need and often desire *participation*, the opportunity to take part in constructive community efforts, to work, and work hard, for the welfare of others.

A TYPICAL WEEKEND WORK CAMP

Here is what happens on a typical weekend work camp in Philadelphia. Friday evening is get-acquainted time. Camp is located in a settlement house, church basement, or community building in one of the neediest sections of the city—an area of religious and racial tension. Campers fifteen years of age and

older come from high schools and colleges and regular jobs—
sometimes alone, often in delegations. A delegation from any
one source is limited to four in order to avoid cliques and to
leave room for other groups. Campers are encouraged to come
from as many different religious, economic, educational, and
racial backgrounds as possible, for much of the enrichment to
the individual comes from other members of the group. The
ideal size for a group is from 12 to 15, but groups of up to 20
can achieve a deep experience of community in just a weekend
if there is an adequate proportion of veteran campers in the
group.

First arrivals help with supper preparation, late arrivals help
with the dishwashing, and all help with eating the food. Often
each person is asked to find out during supper all that he can
about the person on his left so as to make a suitable introduc-
tion of this new friend to the whole group afterwards. Often
first names are learned by the game of adding links to the
chain. One camper gives his own name, the next repeats the
name of the first and adds his own, and each camper repeats
the names preceding and adds his own until the circle is complete.

After dishes there is an hour or more of some handiwork
for overseas relief—knitting, sewing, or doing "Weave-Its" (a
weaving process learned quickly by anyone when Weave-It
looms are available), while discussing informally the purposes
and possibilities of the camp. Often a leader from the neighboring community is a resource person for this discussion to
answer questions about the neighborhood and its problems,
and almost always the discussion is topped off with a song
or game or walk in the neighborhood before retiring. Folding

cots and blankets are provided, but campers bring their own sheets as well as towels and soap.

Saturday is a full work day. During breakfast the work projects are explained and simple directions for the work are given. Afterwards there is a brief fifteen minute period of silent meditation, interpreted in advance as an opportunity to seek the spirit so often needed in the homes to be visited as well as in ourselves. The group is then divided into teams of two (a veteran camper accompanying a beginner whenever possible) and sent off with hands full of buckets of paint and plaster to the homes where tenants have invited "the Friends" to help them in plastering and painting, and where the owner (or the tenant) has been persuaded to supply the materials. It is essential, for the experience to be fully meaningful for the tenants and for the campers, that the tenants *co*-participate as much as possible in the work. Otherwise it is charity work, which experience has shown to be spiritually unhealthful for all concerned. It is in the comradeship of the common work that basic understanding and appreciation are achieved.

Obviously, considerable prior negotiation with the tenants and owners is necessary to make possible work opportunities in five or more homes each weekend, but the results are worth it. Almost always the work is limited to the removal of old wall paper, the patching of the plaster, and painting, although sometimes broken windows are replaced and steps or floors repaired. Throughout the day the work supervisor circulates among the different work projects to coach amateurs, to replenish supplies, and to meet emergencies. Wall papering is beyond the skill of most work campers and is not undertaken unless the tenants assume full responsibility for this work. Occasionally special work projects are agreed upon, such as helping in a community clean-up campaign or painting in a needy nursery or hospital, but this is only truly successful when members of the community participate.

The volunteers return to the camp at midday, as eager to tell of their experiences as to eat their soup and sandwiches. Those teams finishing early are given the addresses of houses where the work is going slowly, so that all rooms are completed and cleaned up by 5:00 P.M. if possible. The cleaning of the paint brushes (as well as the campers!) is next, so that everyone is usually ravenously ready by 6:15 for supper. What happens after supper depends upon the rapidity with which the group recuperates, but often a lively discussion or song-fest is held and is finished off with a still more lively square dance. It is possible that significant discussion or recreational programs can be arranged with members of the neighboring community, but this should not be undertaken without adequate leadership and planning.

Sunday morning is more leisurely, as the discussions of the night before often last after "lights out." Almost always the group scatters to visit churches or Quaker meetings. Those who visit churches in the immediate community are usually most appreciative of the opportunity, often experiencing worship services far more real, more sincere, more meaningful than they had known before. Lunch provides the final breaking of bread together, and the atmosphere of comradeship, sometimes gay, sometimes serious, is often memorable. It is not necessary to have formal evaluation to assure important conclusions being reached. When time does come to break up—and clean up—the camp, one thing at least the campers are sure about: "It is better to light a candle than to curse the darkness."

ONE-DAY PROJECTS

Work projects lasting Saturday only, or even Saturday afternoon only, require much less leadership (as well as much less equipment) than weekend projects, and yet certainly many educational values can be achieved, even in one day. This is particularly true if the volunteer group comes from one source (that is, one school, campus, or church) and the members have other opportunities to anticipate and to evaluate their work experiences. Even so, the maximum length of time possible should be devoted to the project, and preferably it should be started with a meal, orientation, discussion, and meditation before the work begins. For such work days, community service projects such as painting a church or settlement house may be easier to arrange than work in homes, but they may well be disappointing if no members of the community participate.

It is clear, however, that even an entire weekend is none too long for an experience that will affect the deeper levels of the campers' motivations, especially for those being recruited for a service venture for the first time. It is possible for the prejudices of the volunteers to be reinforced (instead of being overcome) by too brief an exposure. It is also possible for campers to be insensitive to the feelings of tenants and to do more harm than good unless coached before and after. Finally, it takes time to grow, and the happy cooperative living and searching and sharing together are essential supplements to the work experience for the most satisfying and lasting results.

INTERNATIONAL WORK CAMPS

Work camps have proved excellent institutions in enlivening and deepening school affiliations such as those described in

182

Chapter 7, "Affiliations Between Schools of Different Countries". Several affiliation work camps have been conducted in France and Germany, beginning in 1950. They are held during the summer, with several students from American schools joining with students from partner schools in Europe. Under carefully selected leaders, they engage in hard labor for the benefit of others.

No outgrowth of an active affiliation requires more prolonged detailed planning than the work camp. Twenty-five campers including at least one teacher for each nationality is large enough. An extra orientation course for four months before sailing and continuing on shipboard is a desirable preparation. The selection of a healthful location and a work project beneficial to others is a most difficult problem, taxing the best judgment of experienced campers. There are no established funds to finance so new an approach to international understanding. Each school has to find the amount that is needed by its own representatives. The responsibility as ambassadors of goodwill in a labor gang, living under camp conditions, with no one language understood by all, requires selection of mature participants. In schools in the United States, both faculty and pupils serve on selection committees. Parents are deeply interested and want to know all about it. Sailing dates, reservations, and equipment are as important as to all other travellers.

One of the first camps was located in a German village in the Sauerland. The job was to help the Lutheran pastor improve the facilities for children and aged among the expellees from the East for whom the village had been required to provide homes. It was hard manual labor, digging a reservoir on the mountainside, and trenches for pipes. There was work in

Figure 27. A work camp in Finland. Courtesy of the American Friends Service Committee, Philadelphia.

the kitchen to be shared and the daily responsibilities of caring for little children. Councils elected by the boys and girls from their own ranks administered the daily life of the camp. These councils never forgot that the work on their projects was foremost, but they also were fully alert to educational values. The spirit of the camp and personal adjustments among the campers were accepted as part of their responsibility.

A later German camp included four French boys. France had not been represented the previous year. Only one of these lads could converse in English. Bad weather and illness made the two opening weeks difficult. Returning to France after five weeks, the four boys called on the School Affiliation Service staff visitor in Paris. They told her of the slow start, of the third and fourth weeks filled with hard work and normal activities, of the fifth week filled with "frictions." They called

it a soul-searching experience. Frank exchange of opinions revealed that misunderstandings were rooted in stereotyped
opinions taught to children as national attitudes. As a result,
the sixth week was "marvelous." "Without these exchanges of
ideas," said a French boy, "certainly the old hatred would
have continued. Our understanding of the Americans was also
deepened and at the end we were one solid group."

The spiritual power of aiding adjustments and reconciling
differences is the mark of a successful work camp. It arises,
in part, from the bond of affiliation between partner schools.
Though young and inexperienced, the boys and girls are conscious of a fine loyalty to their schools. The many experiences
which they have had as participants in affiliation and their
clear recognition of affiliation as school policy raise them to a
high level of readiness for new understandings. They are aided
by the environment in which they work. In the work camps in
the Sauerland, the friendliness of the aged refugees, the keen
interest of the children in them, and the presence of the great
soul of the pastor were influential. As in all American Friends
Service Committee work camps, an opportunity for worship
after the manner of Quakers was afforded. The meetings were
held at dusk after the tasks of the day were completed. Campers sat in a circle with a single candle on a table in the center.
The influence of the silence covering the informal mixing of
meditation and prayer united the group and released a new
spiritual insight and power. A German boy in 1950 wrote:
"Every evening we were strangely moved when our eyes
focused on the tiny flame in our midst. Pleasant and earnest
thoughts circle around it magically. We looked at the candle
and in its glow recognized better than at any other time, our
mysterious existence and our real destination."

A Quaker boy wrote: "Although we meet for a bare 15 minutes a day, we all get much help from our worship. Most of our meetings are silent, but in silence there is unity and meaning. I now feel more than ever that if the leaders of the world could get together in such a work camp and do as we do—work our guts out, talk until we can talk no more, share until everything is done and most of all, sacrifice our personal desires for the good of the group—peace and harmony would result."

The German girls summed up their experience as follows: "We came together in order to strengthen the bonds between our schools, in order to help needy people, and to demonstrate to those around us that young people of different nationalities are ready to use their cooperative efforts in the cause of world peace.... This work gave us much pleasure and inner satisfaction because we had accomplished something positive. In the camp we not only helped others but profited inwardly ourselves through the widening of our horizons. In the crowded life in a camp community, we learned to respect others more, to look out for them, to understand them, and thus to lose some of our egotism. The many discussions with people that came from an entirely different way of life, and thus with a different interpretation of life, stimulated us to reflect, to compare, and to draw our own conclusions."

EVALUATION OF WORK CAMPS BY PARTICIPANTS

Do the participants find work camps rewarding? The quotations contained in the preceding four paragraphs suggest the answer to this question. Other typical evaluations follow:

186

Work Camps

"Why didn't someone hit me over the head and drag me off to work camp long ago?"

"I never knew what real fellowship was until I saw it in action at work camp."

"I was so terrified by my first Weekend Work Camp experience that I didn't come back for three years! I was terrified not by the conditions of the slums but by the challenge of the work camp to my personal and selfish values."

"I still consider it my most unforgettable experience."

"The camp will be for me one of the most joyous experiences in my life."

"I came again primarily to make myself more honest when I said that I not only tolerated or understood my fellowman, but loved him. Once more the work camp helped."

"I think of what work camp did mean to me, and how it has changed my ideas, my thinking, and actually my whole outlook on life. Here at school we are taught how to live a good and satisfying life doing God's work, but until one goes to a weekend work camp you can't actually have the thrill of really living that way."

School administrators and parents have written with equal appreciation. The head of one school states: "Almost without exception, both the pupils and the parents of pupils who have participated say that this is the most valuable single experience in an educational career." Another school administrator has written: "I believe the work-camp to be one of the most valuable educational experiences students can have. My enthusiasm for these experiences has been bolstered by the growth I have seen in my students who have participated, in the knowledge they have gained from first-hand experience, in their understanding and appreciation of the problems of others, and in the

187

satisfaction gained in such opportunity to contribute to the welfare of the others."

EDUCATIONAL VALUES

The following are some of the educational aspects of a work camp experience. Although not all campers derive the same benefits, almost all feel that they have grown and learned from the experience in new and different ways.

(1) First of all, most campers appreciate the joy of simple living, of roughing it, of cooperative housekeeping and informal recreation, with everyone participating and not just watching.

(2) Some campers discover the satisfactions of doing needed dirty work, of learning new manual skills, and of feeling "dog-tired" at the end of a day spent helping somebody else.

(3) Many campers discover substandard living conditions that they never knew existed before.

(4) Almost all discover unanswered questions of economics, politics, and religion. The purpose of leadership should be to draw out those questions and to help the entire group search for answers.

(5) Equally important (and not often discovered by those who simply go on a housing trip), campers often perceive within themselves a basic sympathy and respect for those human beings who are caught in conditions which would discourage the best of us.

(6) With repeated work camp experiences, this basic sympathy may well develop into a feeling of belonging, a feeling of equality, a feeling of solidarity with those who are exploited,

and awareness of the truth expressed by Meister Eckhart: "A joyful heart filled with love is everywhere at home."

These values are best achieved when the camp as a whole is recognized as a testing laboratory, a chance to try out in practice (perhaps for the first time) principles of living too often neglected or discarded, principles of brotherhood and cooperation, which our generation may well *have* to learn.

LEADERSHIP

To achieve these values, it is most essential to have adequate and qualified leadership, and this is often difficult to obtain. To some extent, leadership can be shared. In fact, it is much the best when it is shared. Several volunteers can help arrange the work projects in advance and supervise them, several others can plan the menus and purchase the food, and all can share in the housekeeping and group life. However, unless there are those able to give whatever time is necessary in advance as well as able to draw the group together in a meaningful experience during the camp period, it would be better not to start.

Each work camp is a creative entity in itself, a unique experience of community, a unique educational opportunity. The best results are not achieved by rigidly following a program or a set of rules. Rather, they are achieved by being responsive to the promptings of the spirit of love and truth and life which is in each one of us, ready to lead us, ready to unite us, whenever we give it a chance. This spirit the world needs. This spirit the work camp cultivates.

SUGGESTED READING

Holland, Kenneth and George L. Bickel, *Work Camps for High School Students*. Washington, D. C.: American Council on Education, 1941. Pamphlet.

Pickett, Clarence E. *For More Than Bread*. Boston: Little, Brown, 1953. Part IV, Chapter 2, "Service Opportunities for Youth."

Richie, David S. "Working Together in International Work Camps." *Education for a World Society*. Eleventh Yearbook of the John Dewey Society. New York: Harper, 1951. Pp. 105-118.

Riecken, Henry W. *Volunteer Work Camp: a Psychological Evaluation*. Cambridge, Massachusetts: Addison-Wesley Press, 1952.

"Ten Years of Concordia: International Youth Camps." *Times Educational Supplement* (London), October 17, 1952, p. 845.

9

World Understanding in the Curriculum

RALPII C. PRESTON

Education for world understanding has grown be-
yond the pioneering stage. It is no longer the special
province of a few idealistic teachers and a few dedicated schools. It has found its ways into the curriculum of
schools everywhere, public as well as private, secular as well
as religious. Teaching about the United Nations, for example,
according to one survey, "is taken for granted as a natural and
proper element in the curricular pattern of nearly every school
system in this country." (Department of State, *Teaching
about the United Nations in the Schools and Colleges of the
United States in 1950 and 1951*, pamphlet, 1952.)

I have just completed an analysis of 13 courses of study from
typical school systems in 10 different states. Nine of them provide for the teaching of topics or units with an international
emphasis—the United States as a melting-pot, the world-wide
exchange of ideas and goods, world neighbors, the United Nations, and the like. The interdependence of nations is a common theme also in numerous other courses of study. To be

191

Figure 28. Studying the world. Courtesy of Illman School for Children, University of Pennsylvania, Philadelphia.

sure, formal inclusion of such topics in a course of study does not guarantee better understanding; a bigoted teacher or an ineffective treatment can render such studies abortive. The significant fact is, however, that these courses of study make clear in their statements of objectives and teaching suggestions that world understanding is a major goal.

By way of example, a state course of study in Utah provides a seventh-grade unit entitled "The Story of Nations." It is designed to show, among other things, that every nation is influenced by its environment and that not all nations grow in the same way. Likewise, a state course of study in Florida emphasizes world relationships in grades 10 and 11, and aims to help the students develop world-mindedness, to see events in the long perspective of history, and to recognize our cultural inheritance from Europe and our own influence upon peoples.

Offerings at the elementary-school level are numerous. An illustration may be cited from a Philadelphia course of study. The theme for grade 6 is "Living in the World" and is developed through nine units. One of these, "We Are A World Family," is described in some detail. The course of study states: "Children should learn that beneath the pattern of cultural differences there is a thread of common humanity among the peoples of the world. Instruction in this grade must emphasize that other peoples must not be judged in terms of our own surroundings."

The time-honored study of contrasting regions and cultures of the world—carried out in grade 4 in many schools—has often contributed to a fine understanding of other peoples (though it has also, at times, yielded some pretty superficial, cold, and bizarre concepts among children). Extended study of a particular region and culture as early as grade 3 has been singularly successful in breaking down stereotypes and helping children see how regional differences can add variety, interest, and charm to the world and how similarly humans react despite regional differences. Even kindergarten children are not too young to form an initial understanding of the earth as a globe containing many nations. Possibilities at the kindergarten and primary level are related in the Department of State pamphlet referred to in the first paragraph of this chapter.

A BROAD ATTACK

The preceding chapters have described a wide range of ways in which schools can contribute to world understanding. Ideas and activities have been proposed for use in classroom instruction, for school assemblies, for pupil participation in rendering service to those pupils in other lands, for informal and friendly affiliation of American schools with schools of other countries, and for work camp experiences here and abroad. All these approaches are important, and it is doubtful if the teacher's part in the difficult and subtle task of improving world understanding can be successfully carried out by using only one of them. Lectures alone, for example, would prove about as impotent in this field as they would in teaching an intricate motor skill such as swimming. Fortunately, the philosophy of today's schools encourages a broad attack. It calls for a diversity of school experience calculated to teach, among other things, the simple elements of successful human association—one aspect of which is world understanding. Thoughtful educators everywhere recognize that experiences of an exclusively bookish or intellectual sort would not lead to such a goal. Such experiences contribute a great deal, but human understanding of others requires that the learner be put in touch with others through various means such as those which this book has proposed.

THE INFORMATIONAL INGREDIENT

The indispensable role of facts and generalizations in promoting brotherhood has been brought out throughout the foregoing chapters. Emotional or sentimental considerations alone yield an undependable and ephemeral kind of brotherhood because too often they are not based on facts. Without facts about other peoples, we cannot hope to understand them. Teachers and learners alike must, therefore, select, weigh, and consider relevant factual data. With knowledge, a sympathetic understanding is often achieved.

The generalizations which need to be documented and dramatized through the various approaches are set forth in clear-cut style by Leonard S. Kenworthy in Chapter 2. In essence they are:

> The world contains different kinds of people.
> They are different in large part because they are situated in different physical environments.
> People the world over are similar in many respects, and modern developments in transportation and communication are causing them to become increasingly similar.
> Nations are in conflict, but international cooperation is gradually being organized to reduce tensions and, indeed, several conflicts have been averted through cooperation.

COMBATTING VERBALISM

One difficulty in imparting information occurs when we fail to convey the full meaning of our words to the learner. So he verbalizes—he uses words and phrases with only a superficial grasp of the ideas for which they stand. We all indulge in verbalism at times. It is one of the chief problems of education, both in teaching and learning. Children, engrossed by the fun and magic of words, are natural verbalists. How easily, they discover, their elders are impressed by hearing big words roll off their childish tongues!

Verbalism occurred in the case of a boy who could recite flawlessly and eloquently that portion of the Preamble to the United Nation's Charter concerning the United Nations' intention "to practice tolerance and live together in peace with one another as good neighbors." Yet he proved to have virtually no understanding of what adjustments the preamble calls for in the relation of nations, or even what the term "tolerance" specifically implies in personal living (although he could define it in intellectual terms).

Combatting verbalism does not require activities *devoid* of words; but every effort should be made to see that words are used creatively for the purpose of verifying and clarifying the meanings for which they stand. Each chapter of this book has emphasized the need of having pupils push beyond passive, uncritical learning of words, however noble, and of having the teacher endow empty concepts with content, vitality, feeling, reality, and clarity. These qualities underlie any adequate kind of understanding. Specifically, the chapters have described in detail using personal contacts, films, recordings, creative projects; checking and comparing sources; sharing and exchanging materials with schools of other lands; establishing actual partnerships with such schools; and participating in work camps. These activities give powerful meaning to words and phrases reflecting ideals of democracy and world unity.

One of the encouraging signs of the times is our schools' increasing awareness of the dangers of verbalism. Courses of study stress the need for supplementing the printed word with experiences requiring active, creative thought. For example, the public schools of Baltimore County, Maryland have issued a course of study for grade 9 with a unit entitled "Toward One World" which contains numerous detailed suggestions for stimulating searching inquiry and bringing to this subject a tang of reality. Suggestions include a sociodramatic dialogue, map work, bulletin board arrangements, dramatization, construction of a list of principles, viewing of films, chart making, plans for an assembly, presentation of a pageant, and conducting of panel discussions.

ATTITUDES AS ASPECTS OF WORLD UNDERSTANDING

World understanding consists of attitudes as well as knowledge. Any educational program which confines its scope to imparting information will not influence attitudes very profoundly—although, as pointed out earlier (page 3), a person's attitudes sometimes can be modified by supplying him with information.

Many factors affect attitudes. Let us consider attitudes toward foreign peoples. These attitudes are governed by a person's total mental and emotional "set," which controls his responses to any situation in which foreign peoples are involved. His "set" is the manner and degree in which he is predisposed toward these peoples—whether he accepts them, rejects them, or simply ignores them; whether he acts generously, compassionately, suspiciously, or callously toward them. His set has deep and obscure roots in his individual temperament and personality. It reflects the attitudes expressed by parents and

197

others with whom as a child he had the sort of emotional bonds which make him receptive to their ideas and example. A person's set also reflects his direct experiences with foreigners and the vicarious experiences afforded by reading, television, movies, conversations with playmates, and the like.

Comparatively recent findings reveal that antagonistic attitudes toward foreigners are basically symptoms of an unadjusted personality; only secondary importance can be assigned to reason, ignorance, prejudice passed on by parents or friends, propaganda, and public opinion. (Eugene L. Hartley, *Problems in Prejudice*, 1946; T. W. Adorno *et al*, *The Authoritarian Personality*, 1950.) Prejudiced individuals have been reported to be inclined to blame others for their own misfortunes, envious of the status of others, and suspicious and fearful toward others. (T. W. Adorno, *ibid.*; Gerald H. J. Pearson, *Psychoanalysis and the Education of the Child*, 1954; G. W. Allport and B. M. Kramer, "Some Roots of Prejudice," *Journal of Psychology*, 22:9-39, 1946.)

These findings verify the experience and observation of countless teachers and should give educators pause. In effect, they show that prejudice is in large part a problem of personality, that prejudice remains an unmovable mountain because we have treated it too exclusively as a problem of educating the mind, instead of observing the close relationship between the learner's untutored emotions and his prejudices. It is not enough therefore for us to walk into our classrooms with an armload of books and films and a headful of ideas for stimulating thinking. The problem is much greater than one of intellectual training. The educator must supplement his mind-training role by sharing in the task of re-educating emotions where he finds bigotry and intolerance. The activities described in this book which entail participation in work camps, service projects, dramatics, and other activities involving the total personality all have therapeutic possibilities. For some individuals these activities may prove too little and, in some cases, too late. They may not compensate for situations of emotional starvation during the early years of life in which love and security could not be counted upon. Deeper therapy than the average teacher is qualified to render may be required. The wise teacher will have the realism, insight, and humility to recognize this need in a child and will acquire knowledge of therapeutic agencies which can help.

A person who is not adjusted socially is likely to make a poor citizen of the world as well as of his own community. World understanding and tolerant attitudes grow slowly in the individual, as they have in the human race. They are qualities which require maturity and generosity of spirit. Simple indoctrination about world understanding, therefore, will not produce healthy attitudes. The elementary-school child in particular lacks the experience and intellectual grasp to assimilate meaningfully, except in very limited measure, information about controversial public issues or their significance. He can come to understand simple facts about them, as pointed out in Chapter 2, but the best foundation he can receive for the superstructure of world understanding comes from his daily observation and practice of mutual respect, friendliness, integrity, and consideration for others. The sort of people his parents and teachers are and the way they behave toward outsiders will teach him world understanding and tolerance (or their opposite) far more effectively than what they tell him about world understanding.

Yet we must not make the mistake of thinking that concepts

such as world understanding are solely the products of security and example. The importance of teaching concepts as such need hardly be labored in a book for teachers. It is interesting to note that psychiatrists such as Gerald H. J. Pearson emphasize the need for teachers to build ideals like democracy and international understanding in the consciousness of boys and girls. (*Op. cit.*)

WORLD UNDERSTANDING IN AN ANGRY WORLD

Education for world understanding would be unnecessary if the world abounded in mutual regard and goodwill. The magnitude of suspicion in today's world is education's great challenge. Education, usually obscured during periods of great tension when political and military action assume in the popular mind a monopoly on the key to progress and peace, is actually one of the most potent forces for transmuting distrust and hate into understanding.

Whatever the degree of tension throughout the world, the teacher's responsibility is clear: to help the child find himself and believe in himself; to teach him about the conditions in which the various nations live; to make allowances accordingly when judging other nations; and to consider the comparatively simple aspirations which people everywhere have in common.

World understanding is not world agreement. Nor does it require that we condone despicable acts of individual foreigners or their governments. Nor does world understanding mean passive tolerance—which comes pretty close to indifference. World understanding *does* mean knowing enough about the backgrounds and problems of other nations to know why they behave as they do. Sharp issues are bound to arise, and we are obligated to take a firm stand when they do. When we graduate from our schools a generation of citizens with mature under-standing, we will be as hard as nails for the right and yet able to handle our adversaries with understanding, and we will have made a solid step forward toward national and international security.

SUGGESTED READING

Adorno, T. W., et al. *The Authoritarian Personality*. N. Y.: Harper, 1950.

Allport, G. W. and B. M. Kramer. "Some Roots of Prejudice." *Journal of Psychology*, 22:9-39, July 1946.

Atwood, Wallace W. "Fostering International Understanding." *Geographic Approaches to Social Education*. Nineteenth Yearbook of the National Council for the Social Studies. Washington, D. C.: National Council for the Social Studies, 1948. Chapter 4.

Barr, Stringfellow. *Citizens of the World*. Garden City, N. Y.: Doubleday, 1952.

Dean, Vera M. *How to Make Friends for the United States*. No. 93, Headline Series, N. Y.: Foreign Policy Association, 1952. Pamphlet.

Hartley, Eugene L. *Problems in Prejudice*. N. Y.: King's Crown Press, 1946.

Mangone, Gerard J. *The Idea and Practice of World Government*. N. Y.: Columbia University Press, 1951.

Pearson, Gerald H. J. *Psychoanalysis and the Education of the Child*. N. Y.: Norton, 1954.

Reeves, Emory. *The Anatomy of Peace*. N. Y.: Harper, 1946.

Toynbee, Arnold. *War and Civilization*. N. Y.: Oxford, 1950.

Index

Index

Index